Alexandre Gauthier,
Chef, La Grenouillère..

PHOTOGRAPHS BY
MARIE PIERRE MOREL

Photographs: Marie Pierre Morel
Texts: Annette Messager, Nicolas Chatenier,
Jean-Christophe Planche, Ryoko Sekiguchi
and Laurent Seminel

La Grenouillère: Lizzie Girard,
Emmanuel Roux, Félix Robert, Alix Marquant

Art direction: Folio Factory
Laurent Seminel, Charlène Leroy
Editor: Joséphine Lacasse
Translation from French: Sophie Brissaud (recipes),
Anne McDowall

Distributed in 2020 by Abrams, an imprint of ABRAMS

ISBN: 978-1-4197-4476-1

Photoengraving: Quadrilaser
Printed and bound in August 2019 by Toppan Leefung
Abrams® is a registered trademark of Harry N. Abrams, Inc.

ABRAMS The Art of Books
195 Broadway, New York, NY 10007
abramsbooks.com

As a young girl, I used to visit *La Grenouillère* with my parents. It was always a special occasion for me.

I went to school in Montreuil-sur-mer. Every day after lunch, whatever the weather, we would walk around the ramparts for an hour. The views were magnificent, and I used to stop and stare into the void and at the house where Jean Valjean, the hero of Victor Hugo's *Misérables*, might have lived, and imagine throwing myself down.

Later, on holiday, I spent many evenings (in love for the first time) in Le Touquet, partying and eating Welsh rarebit washed down with lots of beer.

Alexandre Gauthier talks about 'his land', as I do in my work. He's a curious alchemist, who relentlessly pursues his own opportunities.

For him, everything has equally importance: the sight, smell, taste and feel of food – and, I would add, the words he uses to describe it. He speaks marvellously of food – of bread, of the sap of apple trees, of marjoram, of cuttlefish bone, of baby onions – and even his words make your mouth water.

The name of the place, '*La Grenouillère*', reminds me of the word 'grenouillage', which can mean machination, intrigue – or perhaps cooking something up.

The marshland feeds the imagination: it's a place of danger and mystery, of wild ducks, water hens and reeds, of lapping water (and of feminine dampness?)...

Alexandre Gauthier is an artist who likes to communicate his passion. Today, *La Grenouillère* is very different from the restaurant his father Roland handed on to him.

Restaurants and hotels are places that people pass through and where they pass each other, and sometimes places where conflicts or love affairs happen.

Guathier likes encounters and provokes chancy conjunctures in his cooking as well as in his friendships. Ours is curious, unique, he's interested in all visual arts, in Arte Povera, in performing arts.

'What's beautiful is rarely bad,' says Alexandre.

It's wonderful the choreography that takes place here every day: it's a joy to see Alexandre rushing around with his teams in the amazing machinery of their workplace, their beautiful and bountiful kitchen.

His meeting with Patrick Bouchain was pivotal: together, with their combined sensitivity, they've imagined and created an architecture that is poetic, beautiful and functional. What a joy it is to sleep in a one of their huts!

I love this rather sombre phrase of Hervé Guibert's:

'Should not the artist have one foot in his childhood and the other in his grave'.

Annette Messager

-

By hand and by sight

Nicolas Chatenier

I can hold the precious object, delivered by post, in the palm of my hand. It unfolds and reveals itself. I think of the postman who must have struggled to decipher the address written with a very fine felt-tip pen on tracing paper. There is, however, no need for me to look for the name of the sender. This tiny, folded piece of paper is typical of Alexandre Gauthier and his attention to detail, love of materials and passion for beauty. This tiny translucent object contains a whole world. Via this invitation card transformed into a work of art, re is unveiled as a unique place, a source of delights and a space teeming with artistic initiatives.

Gauthier's previous — and first — book was published six years ago, when his company was already cruising ahead. The ship was gaining momentum: it had cast off its moorings and was under full sail. It had great ambitions: to make its way in the world of gastronomy, to establish new routes and to create a different sort of cuisine. Six years have passed, and the vessel has reached its desired port. A second Michelin star has crowned its efforts. The book has made its mark worldwide for both its form and its content. And — the last major project to date — in the centre of Montreuil-sur-Mer, not far from *La Grenouillère*, Gauthier has created *Anecdote*, a restaurant whose gently nostalgic cuisine has established a counterpoint to that of his audacious flagship. At the heart of all these projects is the ambitious Gauthier, who, like a tightrope walker, seeks a precarious balance between precisely chosen opposites.

He has kept his boyish looks — and his indefatigable energy. Animated, always on the go, Alexandre Gauthier remains devoted to his company. Ever alert, giving his attention given to the smallest detail, he is everywhere all the time. Establishing the transformation imagined by the architect Patrick Bouchain, Alexandre is the incarnation of this place, which, while it is rooted in the spirit of his family, has become an eminently personal project, thanks to all the radical changes he has made to it. He lives in this place, which extends from the central hearth of the restaurant to the gardens bordering the Canche on the other side of the bridge. This is his territory — to use a word he holds dear. Here, he methodically transforms everything that catches his eye. He is constantly choosing, refining, improving. Herbs, the vegetable garden, flowerbeds, art installations, landing stages built on the riverside: all contribute to the deliberate and meticulous development of Gauthier's territory.

These moves to improve the place are so continual that they have added an extra dimension to the restaurant we left six years ago. Time has done its work here with style. Like Gauthier, who has himself matured, the decor and the house display a welcome patina. One notices it first on the leather tables and chairs that furnish the restaurant, which have taken on dark, deep tones that add a new comfort and warmth. The spectacular but somewhat severe interior design of the early days has been replaced by a softer atmosphere. The smooth concrete floor has increased in intensity. Mellowed by time and visitors, the materials give the impression of a place that is delights in welcoming guests. In this, there is a radical transformation, which mirrors the maturing personality of the chef. Having moulded the vast array of details that comprise *La Grenouillère*, he seems to have finally created a place that suits him. As though spurred on by a personal endeavour, he has decided to open it up more at the same time as he was opening up himself. Motivated in the early days by personal goals, focussed on his duty to make a success of things for his father Roland's sake, Alexandre Gauthier is now more willing to share, warmly welcome his guests and please others, too.

The other significant change over this time has been as a result of his experiences with the performing and contemporary arts. Although he has always had a keen interest in the arts, this passion has grown since his meeting with Francis Peduzzi, director of the *scène nationale* theatre, Le Channel, in Calais. Thanks to Peduzzi and his intimate knowledge of the performing arts, Alexandre has met a wide variety of people who have changed him. They have inspired him to seek to understand the ways in which artists convey emotion to their audience. The economy of means that characterizes the work of certain artists, such as Johan Le Guilherm and the company 2 Rien Merci, has caused him to reflect on how emotion can be created with little. He has pondered a great deal about this 'almost nothing' that can nevertheless convey emotion. In this, he differentiates himself from French cuisine, which has often neglected the artistic dimension. Here, it is fully embraced. During his travels in lyric lands, Alexandre also met Bartabas, the man from the Fort d'Aubervilliers who has brought about a complete reinvention of equestrian circus art. Listening to Martex (as the troop call Bartabas), he has understood what it is that creates the essence and magic of a show, the moments of which it is composed, the emotional crescendo that needs to be established and that begins with winning over the audience. This grasp of rhythms, this focus on the emotional aspect, this reflection on minimalism are fundamental to Gauthier's current work and to understanding it. We sense that this is a company that pays attention to its impact and for whom aesthetics is integral to its approach. Alexandre offers spaces for artists to express themselves here. From incarnation within these walls, he has passed to installations. It was the workplace of photographer Georges Rousse, who revisited one of the abandoned houses at the end of the garden. The estate's apple trees were adorned with rainwater containers designed by the artist Philippe Robert. The initiative found a new expression in the summer of 2018. Several suites housed in a cottage near the restaurant have been unveiled. These new places offer sleepers imaginary and dreamlike visions. Alexandre has created a new form of hospitality here that gives poetry pride of place. Strewn with this assemblage of ideas, *La Grenouillère*'s path is becoming more and more enchanting with a multitude of discoveries to be made. It is impossible to visit this place and leave unchanged. The magic is being woven even before one sits down to enjoy Gauthier's cuisine: the place itself is inspiring. And this is perhaps one of Alexandre Gauthier's greatest achievements.

But the cooking emains at the heart. It is not a border delineating a territory that is too insular for the creative ambition of its founder. Gauthier's cuisine has been transformed as it has accompanied the evolutionary journey the company has taken. One would like to write that it has become more subdued, but that would not be doing it justice, because it continues to provoke with its bold innovations. In the first book, I mentioned the principle of Gauthier's cherished 'slap', which aimed to leave its mark on the gourmet via a creation full of originality and power. Today, this slap has become a caress. This transformation is reflected in Marie-Pierre Morel's photographs that make up this book. They reveal an intrinsic softness that did not feature in the previous epoch. Shapes have become more rounded, as in the 'raspberry onion' and the 'white radish, cuttlefish ink'. The textures are creamier and lighter, for example in the 'Whole milk blin, crab meat'. The 'iced nettle soufflé' is also exemplary here: it plays with the airy lightness of a soufflé, which is juxtaposed with the thorn-shaped stems that escape from the dish. Soft and spiky, rounded and vertical: the chef continues to play with opposites to continue to throw us off balance. We must therefore never be fooled by Gauthier's shapes and textures: they do not presage an attenuation and certainly not a loss of flavour. Simply, in a desire to share, the radical nature of earlier times has given way to creations that are more complex because paradoxical. This is also a sign of their creator's maturity. He no longer strives to shock at any cost with his provocations. Serene and certainly more confident, he now proceeds by touch or by an indirect approach. Here, we find evidence of the training he has received from the artists with whom he has surrounded himself. He plays with the eater, guiding and leading them.

Never before has a restaurant offered its guests such a global aesthetic experience. Of course, Gauthier will not stop here. He likes to take his creativity beyond the walls of his restaurant for exclusive meals that are also artistic performances. Whether at home or elsewhere, such occasions are full of sensations, transforming this northern chef into a full-fledged artist. Capable of moving and unsettling people, able to enlist different arts, ranging from cuisine to performance via architecture, open to partnerships that enrich him and give him opportunities to speak out, Alexandre Gauthier is walking an increasingly original path. In recent years, he has gone beyond the confines of cuisine to shape people's experiences, make an impact and have his own say. There is no more perfect example of a chef who is so complete that he also reveals himself to be an artist.

-

LA GRENOUILLÈRE

-

There are many wonderful things about my job. The men and women I welcome here are putting their trust in me to help them enjoy a memorable time. They will have planned ahead and looked forward to it, chosen what to wear, taken time out, sometimes travelled a long way to get here, in order to treat themselves to a magical experience. They come, with all their senses awakened, to connect with family or friends, to reconnect with nature, to take a break. In a sense, the clients are offering me the best of themselves: free from the pressures of everyday life and their routines, they are open, attentive, cheerful, radiant.

I love arranging everything, down to the smallest detail, to ensure that our guests have an extraordinary time. We take care of them so that these moments remain engraved in their memory. **What is extraordinary for our guests needs to be ordinary for us, but without it ever becoming automatic, unconscious or routine. Incidentally,** we might wonder whether the ordinary even exists.

Seeking to generate the extraordinary requires us to be consistently attentive to detail but also to remain constantly creative. My daily challenge is therefore to not let up on the extreme precision that cooking requires – despite its more repetitive aspects that can encourage some to take short cuts with details, telling themselves that 'it's good enough' — so that nothing will detract from the high standard of the whole. On a normal day, we create between eight and eleven main-course dishes, six starters, three desserts and two interludes for forty covers. This means 900 servings or small dishes to prepare per service. This calculation may seem very mundane, but it is an essential aspect of our work, which is also about labour-intensive production. We practise a form of luxury **craftsmanship**. For the customer, tasting a dish must be an exceptional experience: either it will be their first time or, if they have visited us before, we need to make sure that the experience is as good as the one they remember. So, I need to ensure that every member of the team bears this in mind. I like to start every morning by shaking hands with every man and woman on my team, looking them straight in the eye so they know that I'm counting on them but also that they can count on me.

I'm omnipresent at *La Grenouillère* and I'm responsible for nearly all areas. I'm at the pass; I'm the driving force, setting the tone and the pace. Everyone knows exactly what their role is. Incidentally, I like to tell people that the service is better during my rare absences. Be that as it may, my main job is to be fully present. For the clients, of course, but also for our fresh-produce suppliers, for a chef who's just starting work with me, and for another who's thinking of moving on elsewhere, as well as for the journalist who's visiting for a few hours. I have to stay focussed and attentive to the smallest details. There's no point buying in exceptional whelks if, due to inexpert preparation, they look ugly on the plate; the most awesome dish loses a lot of flavour if it's insensitively presented.

Cooking involves tasks that are sometimes tedious; a thousand precise gestures have to be constantly repeated. This daily labour is a prerequisite of great cuisine – though, of course, it's only part of the picture. Just accomplishing a task is not enough; you have to be fully present. For example, one of my chefs spent a whole summer assembling a dish of turnip and lobster. I'd explained the dish to him, but he didn't really understand it and wasn't precise enough. With constant repetition, day after day, his work gained in quality, and it attained a kind of perfection the day that he finally took the time to taste the dish he'd laboured over hundreds of times. He suddenly grasped its taste impact: 'It's good ... It's really good ... The balance, the contrast, the freshness, the acidity ... It's delicious!' He looked at me with pride, as though blown away by his own handiwork. What may seem routine and ordinary to us is actually extraordinary.

02

-

VEGETABLE SEA ANEMONE

38

-

POWDERED COD

09

-

GREEN BABA

04
-
CRISPY ARTICHOKE, CHAMOMILE

27
-
CAULIFLOWER,
BEE POLLEN

herbe à
humer
froisser
déguster
l'herbe du
marais
l'herbe à froisser
déguster
Humer
l'herbe

55
-
HERB TEMPURA

29

-

BEESWAX,
YOGURT POWDER

-

I never tire of the banks of the Canche, the ramparts of Montreuil-sur-mer, the light of the Opal Coast. Every day, I enjoy them with a simple and fresh wonder. I grew up here, my son is growing up here, in this place that my father and mother bought forty years ago and I took over in 2003. Territory is a crucial element of my cuisine. The notion of 'territory' is much more open than 'terroir', which is a limiting, almost caricatural word that primarily brings to mind regional folklore and has overtones of unchangeable culinary customs. At *La Grenouillère*, I'm expressing who I am; I'm not simply interpreting a regional culinary repertoire, or even a traditional one. If we talk about the terroir of the Pas-de-Calais, for example, we may think of endives, Maroilles (cheese), beer, smoked herring, juniper... and that's about it. Whereas the territory includes the land, the sky and the sea. And therefore also fishing in the sea and rivers, foraging for food in the meadows and on the beach, market gardening, agriculture and livestock farming. I also like the human dimension of the word 'territory', which for me includes all the expertise. My cuisine is the physical, emotional and mental picture of a season, land, weather and light that is unique to the Opal Coast.

Obviously, we focus on local food networks: over the course of a year, eighty to eighty-five per cent of the produce we serve will have been bred or picked within a forty-kilometre radius of the restaurant. However, I'm careful not to become too cloistered or extremist. My cuisine is individual, inspired by French cuisine but freed from its certainties. This doesn't prevent me from using certain produce from elsewhere, such as pepper, olive oil and citrus fruits, for example. I give myself a framework: with the exception of white and black peppercorns, I don't use spices because that wouldn't make sense here. On the other hand, at Olivier Roellinger's restaurant in Cancale, near Saint-Malo, where spices were traded, it is relevant.

I also have the modest ambition to be a local conscience. My role is to support the business activity of local producers. Encouraging them to maintain high standards day to day ensures my work base. However, I don't want to become the largest local employer because that would cause practices to become entrenched and create dependencies. The territory gives me a wealth of words, a range of notes, a palette of colours with which I can express myself. I attempt to make a fair reading of this territory, in way that fits with who I am, and to be at ease with who I am, without blinkers or certainties. **I see the territory as being a sort of creative boundary for me.**

108
-
FRIED SAMPHIRE
BALLS

12

-

SNIPE, WHITE
SUGAR BEET

Ephémère
humble
unique
UNIQUE
Humble
humble
regard

My cuisine is the physical,
emotional and mental picture
of a season, land, weather and light
that is unique to the Opal Coast.

15
-
RUSK, PEA,
BROAD BEAN

124
-
ELDERFLOWER
VINEGAR

98
-
WINTER RADISH,
BURNT CAULIFLOWER

19

-

PURPLE BRUSSELS
SPROUT, SUGAR

-

I met the artist Anri Sala during a dinner that I created with my teams in Paris, organized by the Chantal Crousel gallery. When my cuisine is taken out of its context like that, I aim to respond as well as I can to the place where I have been invited. In this case, the idea was to introduce this artist to my work by highlighting some similarities with his own. So I went to see his exhibition at the Pompidou Centre. I loved the bubble of glass he had hollowed out in a window overlooking the street and in which he had nested a fragile music box playing the Clash's punk anthem *Should I Stay or Should I Go?* We love music boxes at *La Grenouillère*, whether to accompany a client's birthday or hidden in a very unexpected place in our Maison de la Source.

My transparent ball of sugar recalled his glass bubble: a small symphony of the taste of the marshes echoing a punk symphony. Finding connections is not always easy. I very much liked his installation with gloves turning tenuously, but it brought to mind too clearly kitchen gloves, with which I couldn't do much. Anri Sala's works have a strong sound and digital dimension and it's not easy to play on these aspects with food. However, I was able to offer a dish eaten with the left hand that alluded to the work *Ravel, Ravel, Unravel*, which he had presented at the Venice Biennale and which was based on Ravel's *Piano Concerto for the Left Hand in D Major*, written in 1930.

Anri Sala appeared to be sympathetic to the subtlety of this approach, so I invited him to *La Grenouillère*. He didn't come, and things remained as they were until, ten days later, I got a call saying he wanted to meet me. So, I met him in Paris with his gallerists. Excited by the meal at Silencio, they proposed that I handle the private viewing of the French pavilion at Venice a month later, in May 2013. I made a return trip to Venice the following week to discover the Rocca Palace and its constraints. The logistics were quite complicated: walls that needed to be carefully protected as it's a listed building, material to find in Bologna in a very short space of time, and, of course, the ground-floor wine cellar that would serve as our place to cook.

What had been an artistic project turned into an adventure, a mission to accomplish. The important thing was that it should serve Anri Sala's exhibition, in the truest way possible, and ensure that the evening was a success, and not simply be used as a way for us to show off our talents. We were a team of seventeen, plus the baker Alex Croquet. I wanted to share this moment with him because he's a close friend and as crazy as I am!
The demands of the world of cuisine create some very strong bonds, and we met up again with a friend with whom my father had worked thirty years ago, Christian Bodiguel, who, since then had become chef on the Orient-Express. Out of friendship, he joined his entire team of serving staff with ours from *La Grenouillère* to help us out.

We offered twelve savoury hors d'œuvres, eleven hot and cold starters, eight main courses, fifteen small desserts as well as mignardises and Alex Croquet's breads and wafers. We made nearly everything on the premises in conditions that were nothing like those we are used to working in. Of course, I offered some iconic dishes – crispy chicken skin, weed and brown shrimp salad, avocado and crab, freekeh risotto – but I also adapted dishes to the context, for example changing the marsh bubble into a 'lagoon bubble'. We had some chaotic moments, particularly trying to move around spaces that were heaving with the crowds of people that had flocked to the exhibition that evening. There were some tedious times, too, for example having to check hundreds of glasses. But it was extraordinary. I'm especially proud of the fact that I was able to introduce my teams to Venice, although I regret that only four of us were able to view the work in the pavilion.

There were a lot of human and material factors to manage but, as Jacques Brel wrote, **we spend our lives trying to relive the emotions we felt when we were seventeen years old**, and the experience reminded me of my years in the scouts. Such a challenge requires good time-management skills: you need to be aware, in a somewhat abstract way, of the mass of tasks to be accomplished and fit them into a sequence of events. My assistant Lizzie was a great support in helping me organize everything, keep a broad perspective and liaise between everyone. Her role is fundamental at *La Grenouillère*, not only in the day-to-day organisation but also for this kind of event. The team needed to understand that the evening was not about Alexandre Gauthier but about Anri Sala and his gallerists. The context was not so different from that of a wedding: the bride and groom and their loved ones need to enjoy it. Anri Sala was our bridegroom and it was up to us to ensure that nothing was missing and that he had a good time. People come to La Madelaine-Sous-Montreuil to discover our world, but when we undertake a commission for someone, we're there to serve theirs. This aspect brings us back to the core historical business of cooking.

23

-

CHERVIL, FISH MILT,
HERRING

57

-

Saffron milk cap,
tangerine

20

-

BULBOUS CHERVIL,
HAZELNUT

13

-

COMFREY FRITTERS

83

-

FRESH PEAS, PICKLED ONION

54

-

I'm daily confronted with the proof that my meeting with **architect Patrick Bouchain** was probably one of the most important of my life. With his impressive career — the development of brownfields sites to create cultural centres in Calais and Nantes, his work with Daniel Buren, the Pompidou Mobile, the design of the arts centres in Zingaro, Fratellini, Rostropovich and many others — he had no need to work with me. He also told me that restaurants didn't particularly interest him because he wasn't a gourmet and that this world seemed to him moribund and outdated, whereas 'food is life!' In hindsight, I think I understand why he chose me and agreed to reinvent *La Grenouillère* with me. 'HQH' — **'High Human Quality'** — is a feature of his architecture as it is of my cuisine: it's an obsession we share.

Patrick, with Loïc Julienne, knew how to interpret my instincts by taking me further. *La Grenouillère* was 'green' and it extinguished the landscape. We therefore banned all green. Only black remained to highlight the colour of the outdoors and the texture of the materials: the colour of leather, stainless steel, concrete, steel and chlorophyll. To respect the history of the place, there was no question of demolishing the centuries-old farmhouse, by which one still enters the restaurant today. Guests can still linger for an aperitif in the frog-invaded lounge, which was the dining room in my father's day. We have also begun major building work, and at each service, I'm delighted to note again just what a brilliant idea the two communicating 'marquees' was. The whole space is open to nature, letting in an abundance of light and green; every detail has been meticulously thought out. The dining room communicates with the kitchen, which, while it's not an open kitchen, is a common area. They're two spaces that echo and complement each other. The kitchen is visible from the dining room, which I can see from the pass. This allows energies to circulate, and you can sense the pace.

Patrick has been generous and kind enough to say that you can't distinguish which parts of *La Grenouillère* were his and which mine. Our meeting resulted in a sort of osmosis. I like the comparison he makes between cuisine and architecture. Good products and a good idea are not enough: if you get the cooking or the seasoning wrong, you spoil your dish. The same is true of architecture: it's on site — whether it's a new building or a renovation — that everything happens and the project comes to life. We didn't always agree, and we would challenge each other as we sought to advance the project by constantly contributing new leads in an uninterrupted exchange of ideas. **The time we spent designing and building the place was a revelation.**

The success of a building is also measured by its use over time. I live here with my teams, with the men and women of *La Grenouillère*, but the place needs to continue to evolve. Patrick's buildings are never static; life has real meaning in them, and one can keep moving forward. They are perennial precisely because they are in motion. Many things have changed since the building work was completed — the burnished leather tables tattooed by Philippe Spé, for example — but the spirit remains because **the architect's design incorporated life.**

Patrick also helped me gain confidence in areas other than cooking. He allowed me to spread my intellectual and aesthetic wings. He helped me become aware of my visual sensibility: 'What you produce on the plate, you need to do everywhere here.' He gave me two or three very simple tips, like the rule of the harmonious proportions of the golden ratio, that I can translate in all areas. **I'm listening to my feelings in developing this place he built with me.** I trusted my instincts even further, for example, when designing the three new suites at the Maison de la Source.

Patrick had warned me: the day the building was finished, he would leave the place and I would be alone in it. This, after we had been continually in conversation for more than two years and had had weekly meeting for the previous eight months. In a way, he prepared me for our separation by explaining to me, a long time in advance, that what he'd given me — his advice, his knowledge, his concentration, his attention — was going to be handed over to someone else, because this was the architect's role. His departure created a huge hole. We continue to keep in touch with short messages, but our relationship remains very special. I hope everyone has the chance to enjoy something similar one day.

74
-
GREEN ASPARAGUS,
FISH ROE

11

-

SEA BASS, PEAS

123

-

PUFFBALL

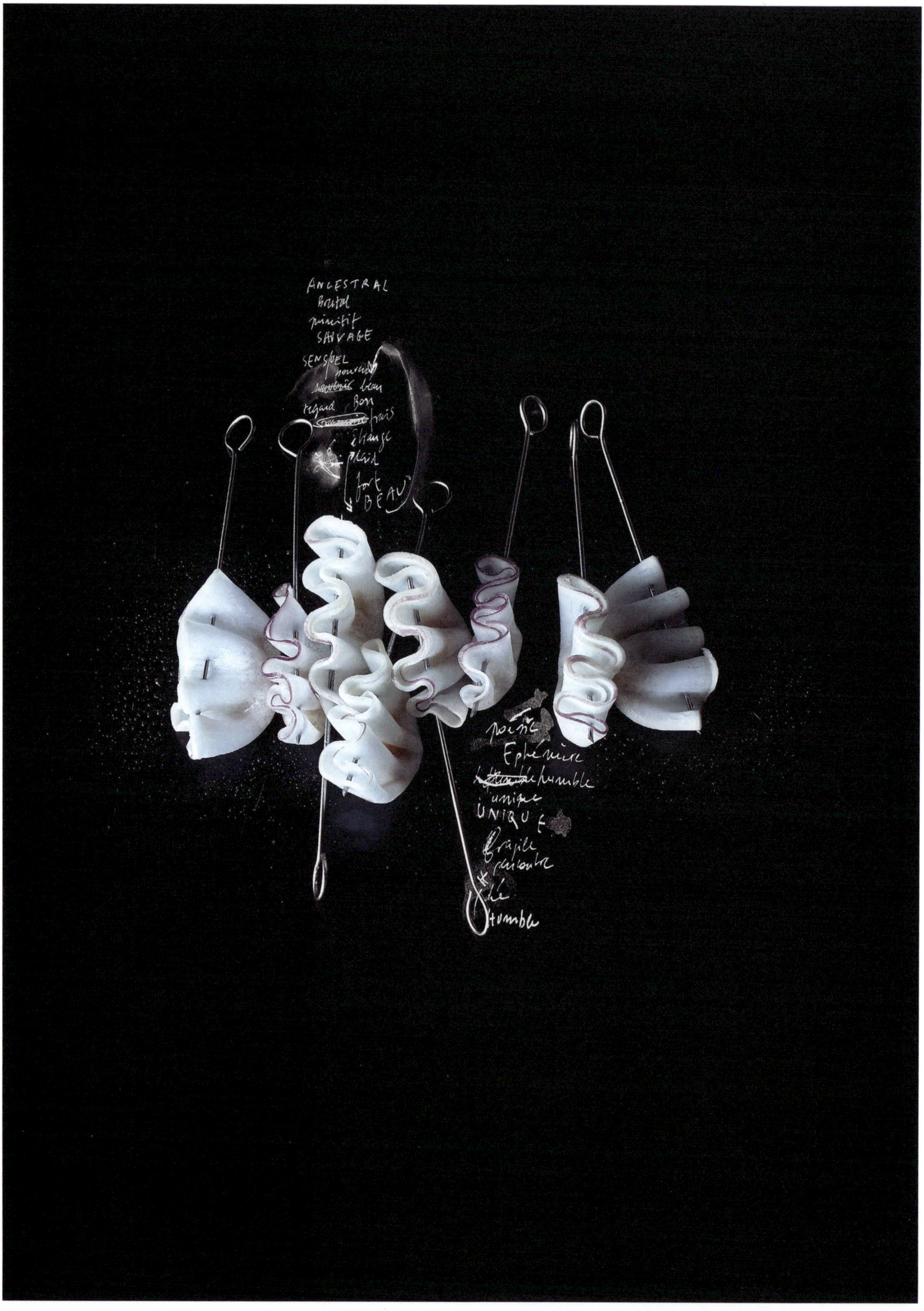
ANCESTRAL
brutal
primitif
SAUVAGE
SENSUEL
beau
regard
Bon
frais
étrange
fort
BEAU
poésie
Ephémère
humble
unique
UNIQUE
fragile
humble

71
-
TURNIP,
COD LIVER

121
-
MILKY
MILK-FED VEAL

SAPERE
promenade
direction
SENS
apprendre
ré-apprendre
inventer
ré-inventer
saveur
d'enfance
saveur enfantine

49
-
SPINACH CAKE

-

In opening the *Anecdote* restaurant in February 2015, I've tried to rediscover the inspiration and identity of my father Roland's cuisine. I was born into the world of cooking with him in that he took over *La Grenouillère* with my mother ten days before I was born. With *Anecdote*, I have transcribed the repertoire he kept in a folder from the time he was an apprentice in Strasbourg along with the recipes he faultlessly typed up, the proportions indicated to the nearest gram: quail with crayfish, pepper steak, crêpes Suzette, *truite au bleu, écrevisses à la nage*. These recipes evoke a cuisine from the past that has been neglected. I wanted to pay tribute to it by reminding people that it's tasty, authentic and delicious, full of simmered, slow-cooked, fresh produce. I've reinterpreted my father's recipes in my own way, adapting the seasoning to current tastes and modernizing the way they are presented on the plate. This nostalgic cuisine is all about rediscovering lost tastes. I'm part of a sort of tradition, but without the negative connotations of being backward-looking and stuck in the past that are often associated with the term. The musician Gustav Mahler, who I much admire, expressed it in these fine and powerful words: **'Tradition is not the worship of ashes, but the preservation of fire.'** *Anecdote* seeks to preserve the fire.

It is also an everyday cuisine. With *Anecdote* and *Froggy's Tavern*, my other restaurant, which is a contemporary carvery, I meet other desires, at other times. These places are the constant link with my territory and with those who live there. I want my cuisine to remain accessible.

Anecdote is also a **tribute to my father's cuisine**. When, bitterly disappointed by the loss of his Michelin star in 2003, he asked me to take over his restaurant, I accepted only on the condition that I could change everything, because the place was not really working anymore. I also needed to discover and affirm my own identity. Twelve years later, when *La Grenouillère* was more established, I was able to pay him the tribute he deserves. Although I had to put it to one side in order to express myself, there is no reason for my father's work, which was so legitimate at one time, to disappear. For me, the idea of **family legacy** is crucial. It would have been inconceivable to me not to take over my father's restaurant when he asked me to, and I have worked hard to gain the freedom and trust that he gave me.

It was in my father's day that the business of cooking was hardest. This was the seventies, when the majority of chefs were tyrants. Cooks were subject to the customers, the restaurant manager and the chef. Nouvelle cuisine began to free us from this sometimes excessive severity. *Anecdote* is a sort of acknowledgement of my father, who began his apprenticeship at fourteen, never had a summer off when he was working as a chef, and yet found himself, despite all the work he had put in for thirty-five years, on the verge of losing everything at the age of fifty-three. Although **I believe it is a fine profession, I am daily aware of how precarious and harsh it can be.**

52
-
LARGE WHITE
ASPARAGUS,
LOBSTER SHELL

72

-

TURNIP, LANGOUSTINE

51

-

GNOCCHI, LEMON,
GOOD-KING-HENRY

30
-
PUMPKIN,
SEA BREAM

18
-
GRILLED BROCCOLI,
SMOKED HERRING
DROPLETS

39

-

FRESH FARMER'S
CHEESE MOZZARELLA,
STURGEON ROE

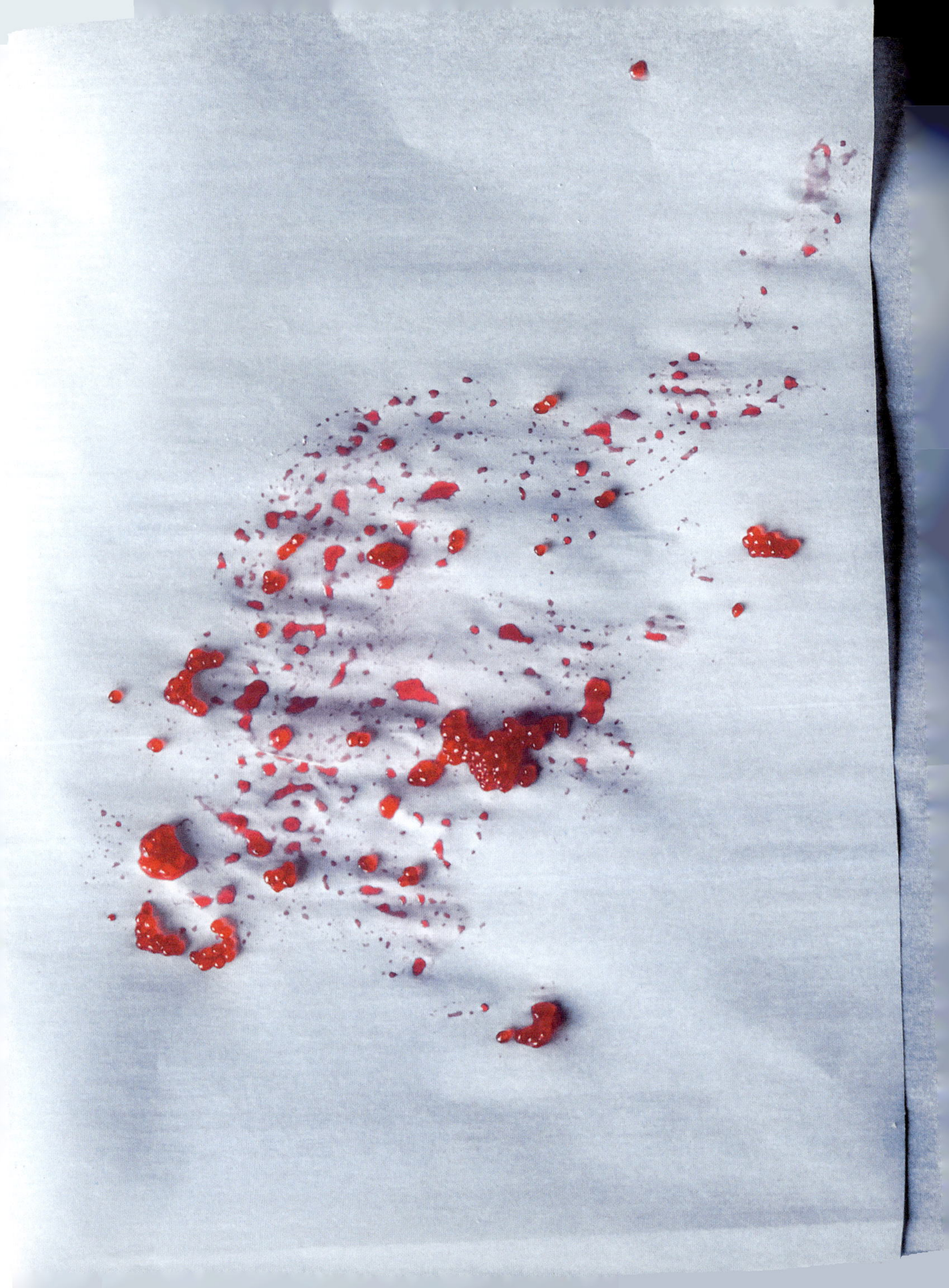

Each season, I take a new approach
to exploring a product, but I don't remember
all my recipes or how I presented them.

28

-

LONG CHOUX PASTRY,
GRILLED BROCCOLI

70

-

TURNIP
CAPSULES

104
-
GREENGAGE

61
-
LANGOUSTINE
BROTH AND CLAW

-

I discovered Georges Rousse through art magazines and some catalogues and gradually became familiar with his work. In 2008, Actes Sud published *Georges Rousse: Tour d'un monde, 1981-2008* and I then realized the importance of his work and the way in which his interventions move me. This big tome became my favourite book for years. I love his works, which I can tirelessly peruse with the same sense of discovery, each time observing new details. But something had to happen to prompt our meeting. We had just bought a house right next to *La Grenouillère* that had belonged to a lady who had lived there all her life: Denise was born in the house and she died there. This old house at the end of the garden was too dilapidated to be left as it was, but before converting it, perhaps turning it into a bathroom one day, I wanted to keep a record, a memory of its history. I decided that we needed to do more than simply document it in some way and so I wrote a letter to Georges Rousse. It took me a fortnight to write, as I carefully chose my every word to express to him the admiration I had for his work. He accepted my invitation to create an installation in Denise's house during the month of August 2015.

Georges Rousse's art is very unique. He defines himself as a photographer, but his work also involves an intervention on the architecture of the places he occupies, which are often abandoned spaces in which he causes shapes to take on physical form by painting their volumes. This form becomes apparent only in the vision his camera offers him, following the principle of anamorphosis. The first work that Georges Rousse revealed in Denise's house, by applying thin silver leaves to the barn, was a silvery circle that seems to be floating in the roof beams. During his second week here, he created an installation in a small room of the house, covering its walls, fireplace, floor and ceiling in a monochrome grass-like green. Day after day, we witnessed his images coming to life. Whenever I was able, I would hurry to the bottom of the garden to greedily discover the latest development in his work. Georges Rousse spent several days at *La Grenouillère* and our meetings were also on a personal level. I was touched by his extraordinary humility, his discretion and his generosity. And I was impressed by his determination to reveal the shape he has in his mind before photographing it. The photographs he takes are, for him, the culmination of the work. Those resulting from the work he carried out in Denise's house are currently on display in the breakfast room. In the first picture, he has preserved in a square an area of the old house that seems to emerge from the green with which he has completely covered the rest of the building. In the second, the square becomes white, while in the third photograph, it finishes as a green square on a green background. This evolution towards the purity of tone on tone fascinates me.

I believe that artists have a vital role to play, but I have no intention of transforming *La Grenouillère* into a centre for contemporary art. **Art is more like a daily inspiration.** I am passionate about pioneering artists, those who have witnessed an era and transcended it. I love abstract artists – Miró, Alechinsky, Giacometti, Caesar – new realism, Robert Combas. Arte povera, too, particularly Giuseppe Penone. I am fascinated by Gerhard Richter and Marlène Mocquet, whose works evolve constantly, in complete freedom, in accordance with their desires. True artists create something and progress in a unique way, unlike artisans, who make use of existing techniques. I don't consider myself an artist but, like an artist, I depend on my imagination, on my ability to create and constantly reinvent myself. I've experienced the joys of inspiration but also know the pangs of constant uncertainty that keep me moving forward. What I retain from the artists I admire is their willingness to pursue their ideas without abandoning their convictions. One of Claude Lévêque's neon installations says: *'Nous irons jusqu'au bout'* (We'll go all the way). You have to keep your course, never compromise. Live-performance artists such as Johann Le Guillerm, 2 Rien Merci, Bartabas and Ariane Mnouchkine are also very important to me. They nourish me. I'm very fortunate that great creators like Annette Messager, Georges Mathieu and Julien Gosselin live or have lived in the territory that is also my own. This geographical proximity has meant I've had the joy of knowing them personally, but also of being on the same wavelength as their art, because, in a profound way, we share the same sensory experiences.

I seek to add an artistic touch to every area of my life. For example, I was trying to avoid manufactured crockery and I was lucky enough to meet a local ceramicist, Sylvie Himpens (her artist name is Syl), who has a studio in Boulogne-sur-Mer. When she came to see me for the first time, I explained to her that I was already working with a ceramicist and had all I needed, except coffee cups, which were uninteresting. As it turned out, this is precisely what she had brought along with her to present her work to me. It was too happy a happenstance to ignore and so we began to work together. I'm sensitive to the fact that these objects have several lives: a chipped plate is re-enamelled. Her unique pieces with very organic shapes sometimes provide me with inspiration for new dishes, and vice versa. It's a continuous conversation.

You could say that me inviting Georges Rousse, for example, was very selfish: I wanted to get to know this wonderful artist better and it was a joy for me to do so. But it's not just about that: at *La Grenouillère*, I can't get inspired on my own. I like to share the things that move me, my admiration for an artist's work, with my teams, the people who surround me and who bring this place alive. Almost nobody on my team knew Georges Rousse before his intervention in our buildings. Now, they all know the man and appreciate his work, and all the more so because his way of managing a project is so exhilarating, engaging and open. Everyone was able to have a peek, spend half an hour or more watching the installation emerge, talk with the artist and even participate in the work. **Georges Rousse inspires action. He re-enchants the world and I try to contribute in my own way to this goal** by arousing the curiosity of those who work at *La Grenouillère*.

In the same spirit, I have taken my teams to see Bartabas's shows on more than one occasion. To begin with, it wasn't necessarily their choice, but such encounters happen often, and everyone benefits and grows from the experience, especially me. I can't progress alone. When I want to raise the bar, the whole team needs to step up with me, and sharing creative experiences like this is a powerful lever for us to grow collectively.

67

-

MIRABELLE PLUMS
IN BRANDY

35

-

POTATO CUSHION

14
-
MIMOLETTE
FRITTERS

82
-
SMOKED HERRING
ROE FRITTERS

58
-
MILK, YEAST

99
-
WHITE RADISH,
CUTTLEFISH INK

53

-

MARSHMALLOW,
EGG WHITE

117

-

PINEAPPLE TOMATO,
SEA BASS

103
-
GOAT CHEESE
RAVIOLE,
BEE POLLEN

SENS
l'œil et le palais
le NORD
retour
s'ancrer
Nord
l'origine
ancrage
territoire
enraciner
racines

It's more interesting to work with products that everyone eats daily and knows well than to impress people with exotic foods whose rarity makes comparison with previous experiences impossible. For me, it's much more exciting to try to find new ways of using a simple potato, a strawberry (in season) or a pea, while faithfully expressing their true nature.

I'm not trying to systematically offer 'luxury' foods, either, even though I don't avoid using them, of course. In any case, the boundary between what is considered luxury food and what we see as ordinary food is constantly changing. Not so long ago, mussels were more popular than cockles because they were rare in the wild and were mostly farmed. People were closer to nature, gathered seafood and had vegetable gardens. It was rarer to eat mussels: you had to be able to afford to buy them and that felt like a luxury. Today, we value cockles, which are hand-picked, natural and less easy to find because they can be gathered only in very limited quantities. Mussels and cockles have remained the same foods they always were, and yet their image has changed significantly. The truffle is considered much more noble than the potato because it's rarer, more expensive and we eat it only on special occasions. But if both products were to be removed from the face of the Earth tomorrow, which one would humanity miss the most? Spuds or truffles? The one that feeds us or the one that flatters us?

For me, the importance of a product doesn't lie in its pedigree. **Every product is noble provided we respect it and view it with an open mind.** A weed can also be seen as wild herb; it depends on your point of view. In the first case, you'll throw it out; in the second, it provides food for thought. I work on the assumption that our only obligation as chefs is to produce results that are both beautiful and good. As far as everything else is concerned, we need to free ourselves from preconceptions and certainties, which limit creativity. Who says that an orange should be used for a dessert and a pumpkin made into soup? I always try to approach produce in a new way, keeping an open mind and constantly researching new ideas. I test, I taste, I get it wrong, I start again: it's a natural exercise. Anything can be a route to tackling a product differently. I try to do things that people don't expect. For example, I got it into my head to improve milk-fed veal by making its taste more complex. I made a hand-chopped tartare to which I added a drop of walnut oil and then enclosed it in a kind of ravioli made from strips of steamed black radish. I then coated the whole thing with fromage blanc and fleur de sel, which made it quite striking.

Respecting a product also means understanding it in all its stages of growth and in its environment. Clams, razor shells and cockles are picked seven kilometres from my home: they are sweet, with a sea-air aroma. This aroma is a gift of nature that is part of the essence of raw shellfish, and I need to highlight it. The taste of these shellfish should also reflect the labour of those who have gathered them, often bent double in cold and windy weather conditions. The context is not the same as that of livestock farming. I'm also sensitive to colours, which naturally match the aromas. When I work with pigeon, for example, I want the customer to recognize the animal and we always leave the claws on when we bring it to the table. I cook smothered pigeons to keep the blood in: I raise the temperature without it reaching 54°C (129°F) so that there's no coagulation or creation of fibres. I offer a single, very tender piece that barely needs chewing, meat that has all the elegance of the pigeon's plumage. It's about sensing that these are birds that flew, walked and didn't live in a cage.

My cuisine is dependent on supplies. In winter, it's difficult to find vegetables other than potatoes, leeks and carrots. There are no more mushrooms, it's the end of the season for pumpkins and radishes have become soft. We face the daily challenge of deciding what we can do and whether we can keep going for three weeks with a particular vegetable. Market gardeners don't always understand my needs and sometimes refuse to work with me, although things obviously progress over time. It doesn't help me, for example, that they plant then harvest all their rows of radishes at the same time, because I don't need such quantities: I would prefer to have fewer over a longer period of time! We have had to get to know each other and to talk a lot for them to understand that I'm not necessarily interested in fruits or vegetables that have reached the stage of maturity when they're usually harvested. I use very young garden peas and work with the pods. It's the pod that contains the seed that interests me because it can be replanted, and the following season will produce a small translucent radish like an opaline that I use raw after letting it macerate in a mixture of several different oils.

I want to pay tribute here to the produce and to the men and women with whom I work every day: Xavier Broutier from the Montéchor farm in Montcavrel, Pauline and Jérôme d'Hauteville's pearly white asparagus from Campagne-les-Hesdin, Bernard Nicolaï from the domaine de Moismont, Éliane, Louis, Sophie et Gaëtan Leviel from the Fond des Communes farm, Daniel Forestier's fraises de Samer, Maxime Leviel from the Mille et une plumes, Robert Therry's honey and hydromel, Xavier Helsmoortel's fleur de sel, the mycologist Mr. Levey, Le Moulin de Marie-Claire and its organic flours in Froyelles, and Mathieu and Valentin Vermes's 'royaume de la rhubarbe' located a bit further away, in the Somme, at Saint-Riquier. I also think of André Loer and Fred, who all year round roam the woods and forests - especially their borders - beaches and bays and other trails for us, in search of wild herbs. And of course, I couldn't forget Stéphane Mille, our market gardener at La Madelaine-sous-Montreuil.

My approach is also sometimes thwarted by the norm. To express myself, I sometimes need special sizes. I used to receive huge whelks the size of a fist. After piercing them several times with a knife, we cooked them in stock, then roasted them with salted butter. The shells were stuffed with dried seaweed, which was burned with a blowtorch, and the whelk was served with a thick quinoa cream. Today, I can no longer find these big whelks. They are no longer within standard limits. Obviously, I understand the need to protect products, but it sometimes seems excessive. Fishing for this or that variety is banned at this or that time, but it's legal to make surimi all year round with what's left of the fish, which is hardly good enough to clean your boots with: a coloured and flavoured fish protein paste that's been asepticized of any taste. **I'm staggered to hear about jam or cheese laboratories: that's how tastes disappear! In the process of making standards to protect our society, we're losing part of the roots of our civilization.**

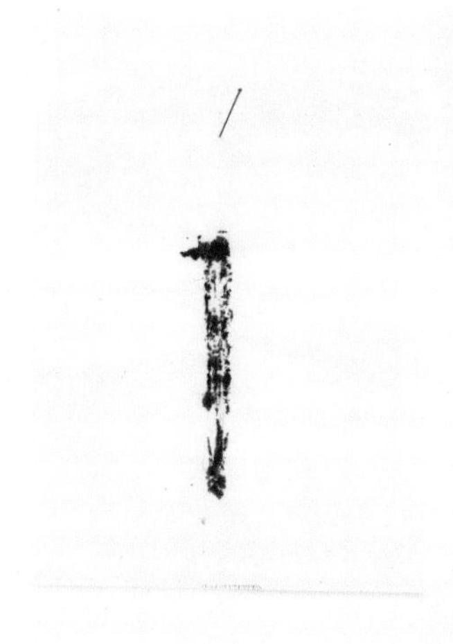

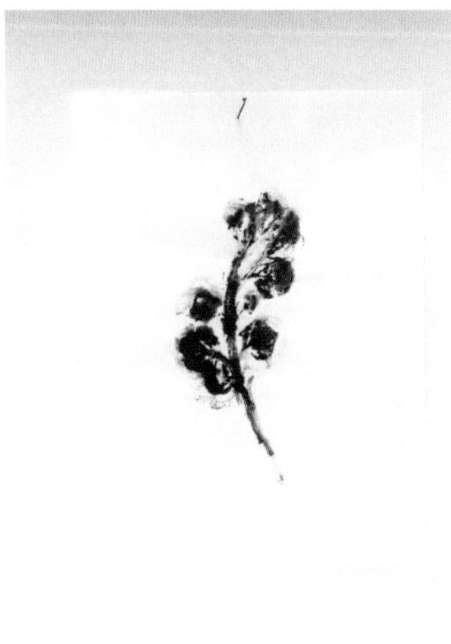

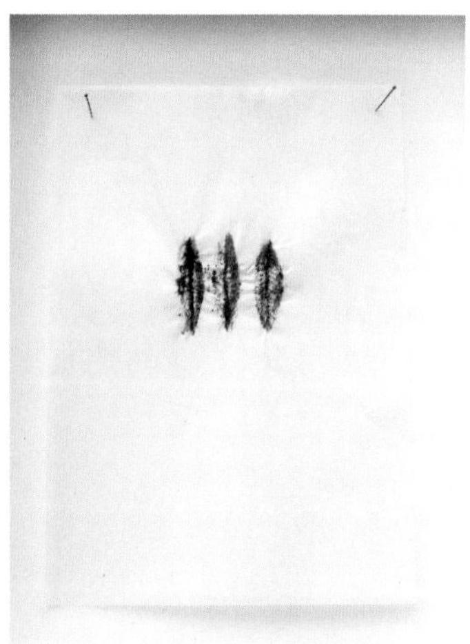

122
-
BEET VERMICELLI

40
-
SWISS CHARD
GREEN, PEACH

101

-

GRAPES,
WOOD SORREL

25

-

BEEFSTEACK
MUSHROOM

120
-
BLACK TRUMPET
MUSHROOMS, LICHEN

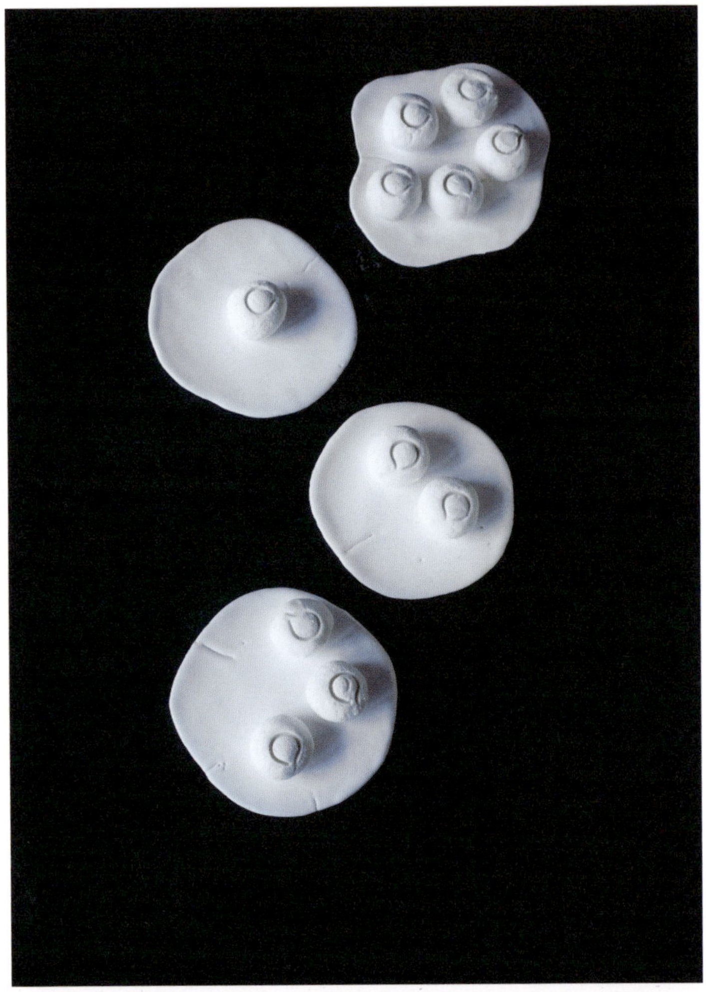

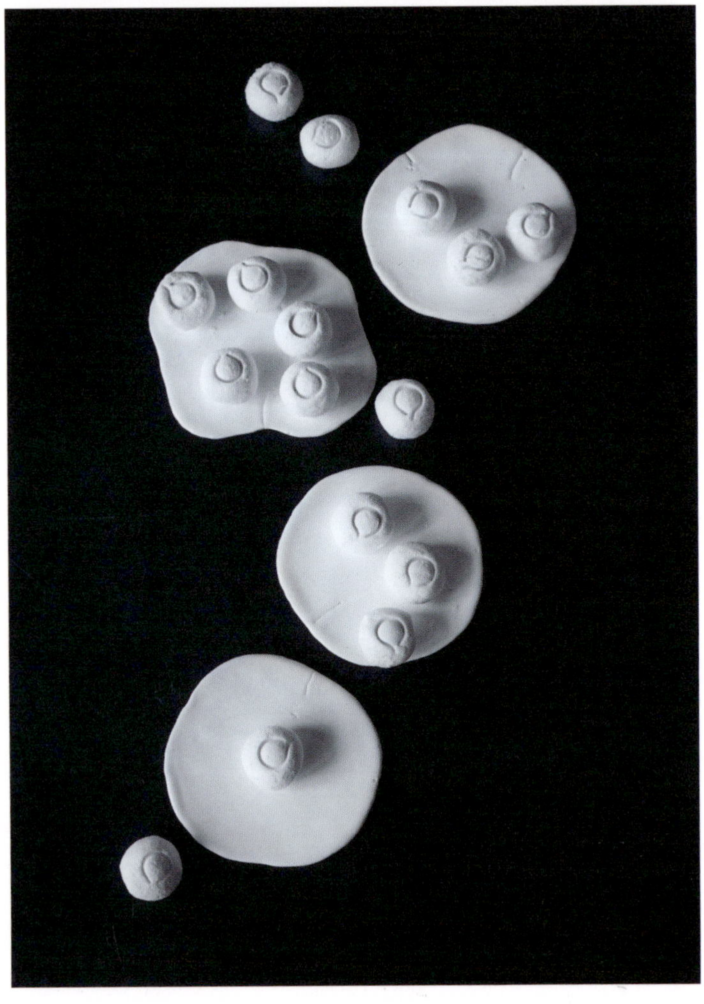

94

-

ROAST CHICKEN

86

-

ALMOND FEATHER

direction
apprendre
ré-apprendre
inventer
ré-inventer

-

I know the Calais well, particularly through involvement with its scène nationale (nationally recognized theatre), Le Channel. As a citizen, I couldn't ignore the appalling situation of the migrants and refugees who flocked to Calais from the 2000s. As cooks are now invited to comment on all sorts of topics, I was often asked what I thought of the Jungle. Obviously, I couldn't say anything other than express my horror, and I wondered what I could do, whether I could help in any way. In November 2015, an association proposed a project to me that involved cooking for the migrants at a free and impromptu concert that was to be given, discreetly, by a world-famous musician. So, I went into the jungle, just for an hour. I have no original thoughts to expound on the subject, no solution to offer, not even a modest suggestion to make. All I know is that the experience has marked me for life. I discovered the reality of which the media can give only the remotest idea. I was going to meet foreigners but, when I crossed into the Jungle, it was me who was on foreign territory. I felt very uncomfortable and very embarrassed. I had entered a shanty town that was damp, muddy, filthy, unsafe and full of abandoned tents. How could I not be a voyeur? How could I help behaving like a tourist looking on at this horror? I was impressed by the organisation in the middle of such utter destitution: alleys, streets, restaurants, places of worship, shops. Everything was organised like I city, but I will refrain from idealising it: I was the presence of mafias, prostitution and pervasive violence and it would be inappropriate to wax lyrical about the ingenuity of the migrants or the 'art brut'-like nature of their structures when they were simply trying to survive and get to England.

I had gone to meet a cook running a makeshift canteen and was considering working with him. He didn't care whether the person coming to cook was famous or not: in broken English, we discussed the constraints — no water other than mineral, no gas for safety reasons — in a completely natural way, between professionals. The project never happened. The association had got ahead of itself; in the end, it was impossible to reconcile the discretion of the operation with the minimum security. I really don't know what to think. I want to take a simple position even if it may seem naive: over and above the various misrepresentations, here was a humanitarian crisis with 6,000 totally destitute people who had been living in such perilous conditions that they had chosen to leave everything rather than stay at home. At other times in history, it was our ancestors who had to leave suddenly and abandon everything because of war. It helps, a little, to imagine what that means for a woman, a child or a man. Quite simply, this concerns all of us, as human beings.

I have a little boy. In the Calais Jungle, I saw young children with their feet in the mud. Barbara sang in *Göttingen:* '*Les enfants ce sont les mêmes / à Paris ou à Göttingen.*' (Children are the same / in Paris or in Göttingen.) I can't help but think that the children of the Calais Jungle are the same as those in Paris — they're in search of a future. I don't want to pretend that everything is fine, even if I feel helpless. Simply put, we need to be humanist. The Jungle also raised the question of how we welcome others. It's not about being naive and confusing the issues, but we welcome strangers at *La Grenouillère*. In the past, when you welcomed someone into your house, you would wash their hands and their feet. For a long time, *La Grenouillère* was the ferryman's house. What do we make of that? **Having a liking for others is essential in my job.** What does it mean to welcome someone, whether they've travelled just a few kilometres or thousands? There's no clear-cut answer, of course, but asking the question daily is already a form of answer. Welcoming someone is first and foremost about giving them your whole and sincere attention.

81

-

POTATO
YARN BALLS

79

-

JOHN DORY SKIN,
ANCHOVY

68

-

LEMON VERBENA
MILK FOAM

05

-

WHITE ASPARAGUS,
FERMENTED TURNIP BROTH

85

-

OYSTER MUSHROOM,
SCALLION

RECEP
TION

-

It all started with the Chef of the Year Award that Gault & Millau honoured me with. At the reception, I met the Minister of Foreign Affairs, Laurent Fabius, who, during the dinner, offered me the chance to be involved with a meal for heads of state. In fact, in December 2015, France was to welcome the twenty-first United Nations Climate Change Conference (COP 21), during which 192 heads of state would gather to decide on measures to implement to limit global warming. For ten days, I heard nothing, then the following Monday, I received a written proposal and a phone call from the director of the minister's office. The following day, I went to Paris. The pressure rose higher still when I learned that I had been chosen to prepare the main dish of the meal, the most prestigious moment. The starter was to be prepared by Yannick Alléno and a garnish accompanying the dish created by Nicolas Masse. Marc Veyrat was to prepare the cheese and Christelle Brua the dessert.

I needed to succeed in conveying my identity as a chef while pleasing 'the whole world'. There were numerous constraints because the dish had to suit the eating habits of all the heads of state, taking into account their religions. So, no pork, no red meat. No lamb either, because the Japanese and Chinese consume very little of it. We concluded that the common gastronomic denominator was poultry, and so I proposed cooking Licques poultry. A chicken supreme, gently cooked 62°C, accompanied by wheatgrass, cooked like a risotto, with chervil and cress. It's a dish that I master well as it appears throughout autumn on the menu at *La Grenouillère* but made with pigeon. Nicolas Masse added braised celery, stuffed with confited chicken thigh. Loyal to my territory, I saw this prestigious invitation as an opportunity to be an ambassador for the produce and men and women of my region: poultry from Licques, raised a few kilometres away, produce from market gardener Stéphane Mille and producers with whom I have worked for years, including Jean-Louis and Maxime Dandre and their wheat from the Moulin de Brimeux.

The event itself was a challenge. All the dishes had to be pre-cooked in Lenôtre's workshops at Plaisir. In the original plan, each chef was to be allowed five assistants but, with the terrorist attacks of 13 November and the subsequent implementation of a state of emergency, I was finally allowed to take only one person. So, it was my assistant, Félix Robert, who went to prepare the dish on the Sunday. I arrived on the site on Monday at half past five in the morning. Nothing had been left to chance. It was really impressive. The security services inquired about each member of the technical staff. They greeted all the chefs by looking them in the eyes, checking for any possible suspicious behaviour. President Obama's security agents were behind us while we prepared the plates. They were not excluding anything, even poisoning. Three plates were assembled, and a bodyguard took one of them. Even the knives were counted! It should be said that during COP 21, the Bourget site became UN territory, with all its stringent safety rules.

I soon understood that we were completely at the service of the event. At *La Grenouillère*, I do as I like. There, we had to submit to all the constraints that the organization of the summit dictated and to its protocol. The service was entirely handled by the staff of the Élysée Palace, the Hôtel Matignon and the Quai d'Orsay, who were highly experienced at this drill. Of course, I was able to enjoy the sight of the dining room before lunch was served: tables laid with the official tableware, Sèvres faience plates stamped with the coat of arms of the Republic. The meal had to be fully served and eaten in an hour and a quarter. It was announced forty minutes late and finally lasted only fifty-five minutes in all. We finished cooking on the premises and had just seven minutes to deliver the 192 plates! Fortunately, I had twenty people to prepare them. The difficulty was, of course, that the dish needed to be served hot but not too hot. There was no question of starting again. Once a plate was sent out, there was no going back. **The supportive atmosphere among the chefs was galvanizing**. We had seen the heads of state when the official photo was being taken but not during lunch. I kept a close eye out for the return of the plates, and it seemed that the dish had been appreciated as they came back empty. Some had left the herbs, and just seven had asked for a vegan menu, which had, of course, been anticipated.

Such exceptional moments are not the essence of my work, but they are important. That I was sought out, in the countryside, in the North, to represent French chefs as a whole, is a real mark of recognition. I feel proud to have been allowed to highlight the territory, its produce and, especially, the producers.

96
-
COCKLE
QUENELLE

87
-
SNAP PEA,
NASTURTIUM

95

-

FIRST PEAS

43

-

COCOA, CLEAR
SPIRIT VINEGAR

03

-

SMOKED EEL

In the past, when you welcomed someone into
your house, you would wash their hands
and their feet. For a long time, *La Grenouillère* was
the ferryman's house. What do we make of that?
Having a liking for others is essential in my job.

109

-

BUCKWHEAT,
SALT-CURED LEMON

84

-

CRAB,
BLACK RADISH

-

I deeply dislike the word 'service' because it carries a connotation of servitude. I prefer the word 'care': we should be helping our guests enjoy the moment, creating something ephemeral, so that between the time we open the door to them and the one where we close it behind them, there's a poetic interlude. This presupposes that the team is happy. There are too many places where people are seen to be 'working' and the professional world of catering has been particularly harsh for years and often still is: tyrannical chefs, humiliated apprentices, the staff confined to chores. Here, there is complete transparency. There are no pans or knives flying through the kitchen to land on the head of the poor apprentice! We spend our lives in this place. My team has come to join me on a project — my life project: to make *La Grenouillère* a restaurant and much more than that. For that reason, I wouldn't expect men and women to work in conditions that are worse than those in which I receive my clients. They spend more time with me than they do with their partners and children.

The kitchen is not particularly standard; nor is the workspace: there are no tiled floors and no ceilings, just stainless steel and concrete. I wanted a kitchen as comfortable as the dining room because I don't want there to be a division in the restaurant between the customers and the staff. In my kitchen, there is daylight of day, space, music, an extractor hood that makes no noise. At *La Grenouillère*, people love their work and enjoy being together; they share their feelings. We decided not to have music in the dining room, but we do put it on in the kitchen. The idea is not only to work with music, because when we are serving, everyone is concentrating and the background music fades out. The goal is to create an ambiance, to offer, but not impose, a sound atmosphere. As a customer at *La Grenouillère*, you can focus on the food, on the taste, but you can also glance over at the kitchen and tune into its musical atmosphere. You see the cooks not only being busy but also moving with the music: it's like a ballet!

I think this idea of rhythm is essential. We serve a dozen dishes, to which are added interludes and amuse-bouche. I don't like long waits between each course. For me, ten minutes is the maximum. This steady pace creates a buzz, a kind of **euphoria of generosity**. Being surrounded by such attention also creates a perpetual curiosity: what will happen next? Creating a rhythm means thinking about commas and even dissonances, a little like in a symphony, or in a conversation, where you don't always speak in the same tone. The roasted chicken ball that we offer between two dishes is a dissonance. It can also be in the dish. I offer, for example, a nest of raw asparagus, grated like carrots and dried, which looks like straw. Inside it, we put some Stilton. The dry asparagus is rehydrated very quickly in the mouth and the marriage with the very acidic Stilton gives a strong taste with a very pronounced bitterness. The start is rather sweet and delicate and then your taste buds are assaulted. We need to dare to change register — like twenty violins suddenly stopping and leaving space for the horns. Dissonance, however, is not the same thing as cacophony and I would be wary, for example, of simply serving a cone of chips that would lower the tone for the customer.

One person takes care of each table, which means the waiter can establish a special relationship with the kitchen and the client. I encourage each waiter to present the dish to the customer in their own words, leaving space for some mystery, of course. I ask them to make use of the evocative and rich nature of words, to consider the difference in **nuance between 'aged' and 'spoilt', a plate that is 'broken' and one that is 'chipped'. A piece of paper that is 'creased' is not crumpled; to 'place' something is not the same as to 'deposit' it. There's an elegance in such nuances.**

97

-

RED ROOT

10

-

KNIFE-CUT SEA BASS,
FLOWERS

116
-
HORN TOMATO,
SEA BREAM

63

-

PRESERVED STRAWBERRY,
HOGWEED

Being surrounded by such attention
also creates a perpetual curiosity:
what will happen next? Creating a rhythm
means thinking about commas and even
dissonances.

89
-
CLOCHARD APPLE,
QUINCE

31
-
QUINCE

La Serre

From the first day I started working at *La Grenouillère*, I've wanted to create a 'restaurant that is not just a restaurant'. Just cooking is not enough: I need to welcome and meet people, and to talk about cuisine in a different way. I never know quite how to go about doing the rounds of the tables at the end of a meal: it can be embarrassing to intrude on the diners' privacy. Conversations turn quickly to the weather, or the diners are a couple who don't want to talk to anyone else. **I seek to establish a different sort of conversation by introducing the world of the arts.** Cuisine is by nature an ephemeral experience: the dish has a life of three minutes. Sitting down for a meal is primarily a shared experience: we rarely eat alone and eating with others can be very sensual. We try to be consistent in the kitchen and at reception, so that we're all on the same wavelength. Le Marais Forain was conceived to create a special time that extends and enriches the act of cooking.

For the first edition, which was held on 30 August 2016, I invited the staff from the three restaurants and their families, locals from the area, artists, important clients, friends and guardian angels and ambassadors of the restaurant. Although they didn't necessarily know each other, these people had *La Grenouillère* in common — they love the restaurant, the food and the men and women who work there — so they couldn't fail to get along! I wanted to invite everyone to be my guests. Firstly, because I wanted it to be a friendly time, but also because when we pay for something, we become less curious: we tend to choose, rank and judge. Being invited encourages a certain elegance; for example, people pay attention to what they're being offered, when they might otherwise have felt it wasn't something for them. I really hoped that it would be a day of sharing and that everyone — artists, cooks, friends and family, local producers — would feel confident enough to be open to the worlds of others. I have a formed a strong friendship with the artist Jérôme Bouvet, who uses street theatre and circus to offer poetic moments that rely on precise and subtle gestures. His performances invite us to contemplate the ordinary things: a snail, a nut, a piece of rope. For him, the beauty of things lies in the way we look at them, and I recognize myself in this approach. Together, we created *Le Marais luisant* (The Glistening Marsh), a culinary and artistic adventure that we presented in the *scène nationale* theatres of Calais and Le Havre.

Together, we also conceived *Journée Marais Forain* (Marsh Fairground Day), to which we invited artist friends. We were very fortunate to have Bartabas, who offered us a 'sunrise' performance with his chestnut Le Caravage on the rampart slopes; Jacques Bonnaffé, who enchanted the gardens with his words; and the Carabosse company, who illuminated the Canche River, the bridge and the path with 300 fire pots and 40 flying lanterns. Over the course of the day and a good part of the night, twenty artists entertained visitors with their wit, games, music, snail racing, tales about cows and a concert featuring fifty-five pressure cookers. The day was also punctuated by meals taken together around long tables. The food was not central to the day, but it naturally played its part in this 'poetic journey of discovery of the territory in every sense of the word'. The sun was shining brightly on 30 August, creating a climate conducive to taking it easy. This suited us, because we didn't want the day to be characterized by frenetic activity, which is the case at many festivals, where people run from one show to the next without a break. **We wanted to leave time for our guests to meet and get to know each other, to chat** and share food and poetic moments together in a leisurely way. The day was not about communicating or promoting ourselves but about sharing. The event was held again at the end of August 2018 and so has become biennial. I can't offer it every year because it involves closing *La Grenouillère* and therefore a loss of income in addition to the high production cost of the Marais. On alternate years, we hold a more modest but just as special event: a meal followed by the show *Gramoulinophe* by 2 Rien Merci, an evening followed by the show *La Serre* by Jean-Paul Lefeuvre & Didier André. I think that an annual event where all the friends of *La Grenouillère* can meet up is essential for maintaining the ethos of the place.

16
-
WHOLE MILK BLINI,
CRAB MEAT

24
-
CHERRY,
GREEN ALMOND

46

-

RASPBERRY

112
-
WINEY SPATULA

78

-

ONION SKIN

75

-

SLOW-ROASTED
ONION ON A BED
OF SEA SALT

poésie
Ephémère
humble
unique
UNIQUE
fragile
rencontre
idée
Humble

34

-

YELLOW COURGETTE,
BEE POLLEN

60

-

BRAISED LETTUCE,
SORREL

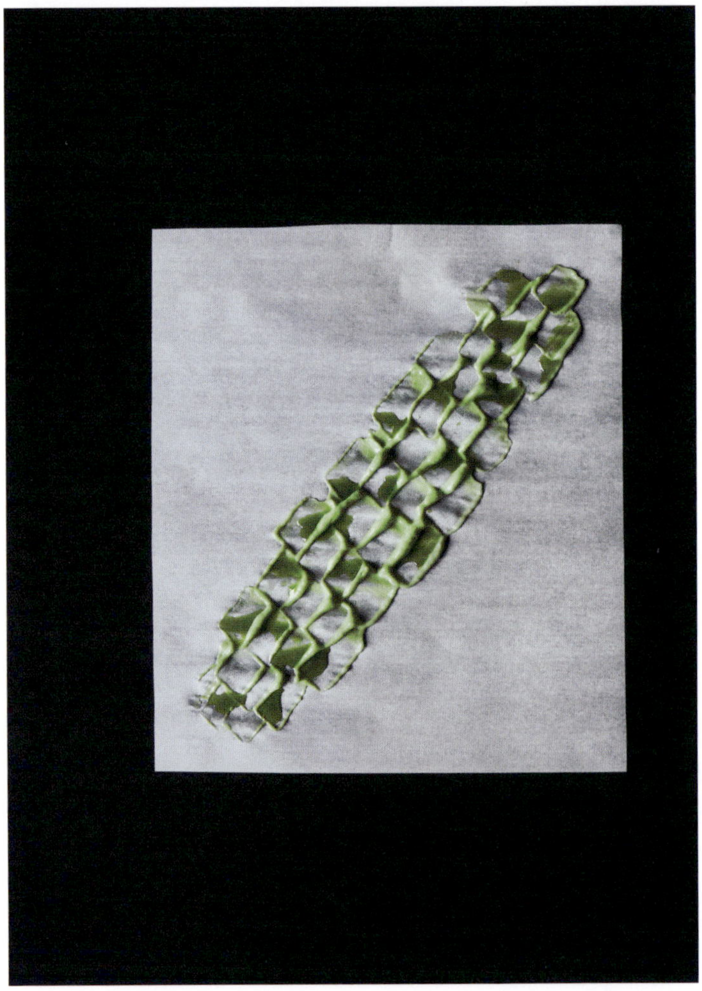

59

-

GOAT'S MILK,
DANDELION

For me, creating a dish is the result of spontaneous decisions, and I find it difficult to put that into words. I work intuitively. I look at works of contemporary art, recall childhood memories, listen to people around me, contemplate nature, and I pay particular attention to the work of architects because a dish is also a construction, and all this infuses and emerges in a dish without me really being aware of the process. I don't have a systematic way of creating. I don't try to transpose this or that aspect of the real or artistic world into a dish. I interpret it in an **intuitive way**.

Some dishes come from a flash of inspiration. I have notebooks in which I write my ideas on the left-hand page and the dishes made on the right-hand one. Inspiration can come from an apple I'm munching, a supplier's list or the shape of a plate my ceramicist has dreamed up. My cuisine requires above all a healthy dose of imagination, although it's essential to understand the ingredients as a whole, and at every stage of their maturity, and that demands a lot of technical skill, too. I try to approach each product in a new way, without any preconceptions. What does an apple become if I appreciate from the point of view of someone taking a nap in the shade of an apple tree? Or a grandmother stewing it? Or its place in a meal? I also play around with food matches. Oyster and vanilla, cockles and clementine, cocoa and vinegar. **I don't need to taste something to know if the combination will work. I imagine it and it's there in my mouth, as something completely self-evident.** It's a cuisine that suits me well: imagined, thought out, created, prepared and eaten in my restaurant. I like bold tastes.

When I create a dish, I always ask myself the same questions: have I eaten it before? Does it have something of me in it? Is it good? Do I want to share it, to talk about it? The secret of a good dish lies first and foremost in its simplicity, and that, of course, is not something simple to achieve! The clarity and the visual reading of a dish are also, I think, fundamental: I sometimes play on trompe-l'œil effects, such as with egg white, marshmallow, vinaigrette made with fish entrails, which have matching textures and colours. My cuisine is very concentrated, with ingredients that touch each other because they're eaten together. I never use more than three ingredients. In fact, some dishes are created with just a single product, such as this dessert, made only from apple peel crisps, of up to seven different varieties, which presents the fruit in a variety of ways, from ice cream to apple tree sap. Each season, I take a new approach to exploring a product, but I don't remember all my recipes or how I presented them.

My inspiration is linked to the products available, as well as to the season, their quality, my mood and other, practical, factors. Sometimes, I'm unable to offer a dish that requires long and complex preparation due to a shortage of staff to handle it that day. My menu is dynamic and is printed before each service. I have a need to create new things all the time. It galvanizes me. I'm also aware — and it can put me under enormous pressure — that it's what's expected of me. I was made a *chevalier* (knight) of the Ordre des Arts et des Lettres in 2012, then an *officier* in 2018, because my cuisine is unique and innovative, and this has become *La Grenouillère*'s identity: it's a place where we seek to constantly forge new culinary paths. Customers don't come here to eat *blanquette de veau*. The same is true of the chefs and waiters: the people who come to work here are hoping for innovation, for the chance to experiment with new techniques. These expectations motivate me and lead me to surpass myself.

For now, I have no desire to offer signature dishes but, over time and with the incessant workload, it's possible that I'll end up finding the most authentic and perfectly finished dish that expresses each product in the clearest and most self-evident way. Occasionally, I say to myself about a dish, 'we've done it': such is perhaps the case with the lobster with juniper or the crab blinis. The writer Milan Kundera sometimes spends weeks writing a single sentence: there comes a moment when it's no longer possible to remove a word or add a comma without weakening it — the sentence is perfect. I'm far from having reached this perfection for all the produce in my territory, but I think that the continual revitalization of my cuisine is also a progression, a daily quest for its essence.

41

-

Chicory dandelion,
duck fat with the knife

113

-

LANGOUSTINE
TUILES

73

-

ASPARAGUS NESTS,
STILTON CHEESE

My cuisine is very concentrated,
with ingredients that touch each other
because they're eaten together.

21

-

CAPERS, TANSY

32
-
CELERY, APPLE

100
-
PINK RADISH,
VINEGARED GEL

76
-
RASPBERRY
ONION

50
-
GOOSEBERRY,
RADISH

91
-
APPLE,
LANGOUSTINE

When I took over *La Grenouillère*, there were still large plates decorated with cornflowers and a complete set of silverware on the table. This decorum was in keeping with the spirit of the famous French gourmet meal. **But is it really a luxury to change knives several times?** Do they cut less well depending on the dishes? I preferred to opt for a single knife, on the table throughout the meal, to be used as an implement. A single knife but a beautiful one, specially designed for the restaurant. I think that's what real luxury is. Michel Bras had paved the way with his restaurant in Laguiole. The new knife we've put into service is the third since I've been here. The first was made in the Jura. I loved the second, which was specially forged for us by a cutler, but it contained metal chloride that seeped into the leather of the tables and so we had to change it.

I met Jérémy in 2014. This cutler has had a very unusual career in that he spent years studying philosophy and literature, has a doctorate in social sciences was even a university researcher before he taught himself to make knives. He is also passionate about nature, especially that of Norway, which he discovered when he was eighteen. He had sent me some knives, but his aesthetics didn't match mine, although his approach interested me. We exchanged emails regularly, but it wasn't working: I found him charming but too indirect. **I always prefer to start by making a simple connection with people, then, once a relationship has been established, to get into more intimate and involved conversations.** To set the world to rights with someone until four o'clock in the morning, I need to have a level of confidence in them that can't be built by ignoring steps. Jérémy came back to *La Grenouillère* for a long time. He offered me a brigand knife and I told him about my connection to the object: my years of scouting; the first knife my grandmother gave me; the name of my son, Eustache, which is also the name of a pocket knife…

The cutler explained to me his fascination with such an apparently simple object: making a knife is about hoping to create a real connection between the future user and the piece you've created for them. This involves taking the time to listen and to understand their aesthetic tastes, their habits and their relationships with others. You need to have a certain amount of confidence in someone to hand a knife to them, in terms of both the care they will take of it and they way they'll use it. In their hands, it can become a useful implement for cooking a meal for their friends, a companion for an outdoor life or a means of defence or even attack. He explained to me that, for him, a knife is neither good nor bad in itself, but that it reminds us of our responsibility for how we act in this world. He is developing an approach that interests me.

We had six months of discussions before we arrived at the final result: three months of designing it, then three months of manufacturing it in Thiers. It's a very small, rigid knife of 143 millimetres in total, which Jérémy called the 'tadpole'. It is very elegant in its sophisticated simplicity: a burnt oak handle with rare veining, with a very technical full-tang assembly. The choice of the small blade changes the distance to the plate and the relationship to the product. The knife is essential for the restaurant as it's used by guests every day. We have it in a range of collection models. I also wanted to produce a very limited and numbered edition that we now offer to all cooks who have worked at least six months at *La Grenouillère*. The unique knife is a token of our gratitude — a very powerful symbol. The real luxury lies in these choices that we make about every last detail. In a world where everything is increasingly calibrated, where we all have the same manufactured products, a unique piece gives true identity to the objects we use. This is part of what gives the restaurant its style.

08

-

AUBERGINE,
COD LIVER

01
-
BURNT APRICOT,
MARJORAM

66
-
SMOKED
MIRABELLE PLUM

93.9

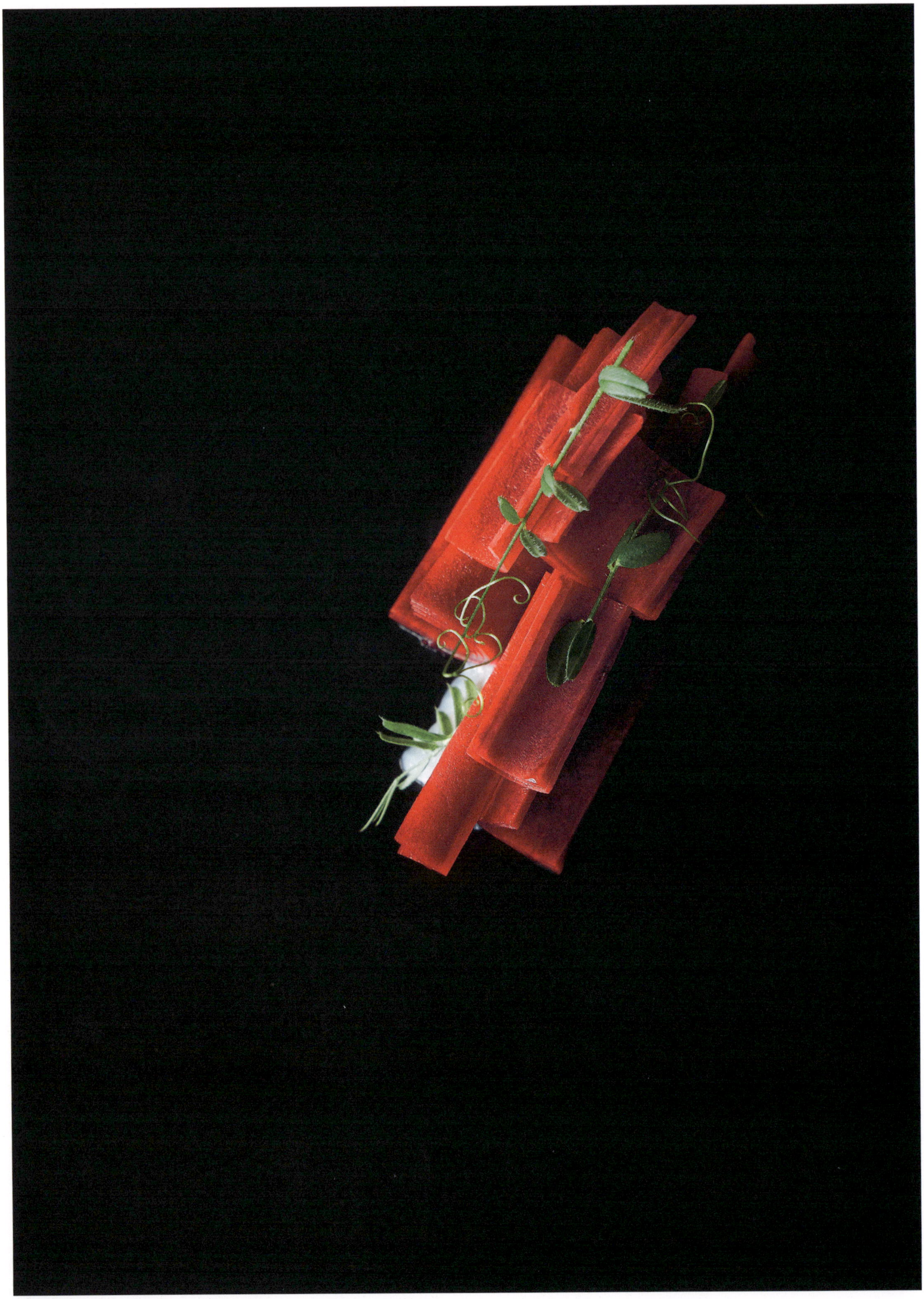

22
-
Purple carrot

47
-
Wild strawberry,
lemon verbena

64

-

STRAWBERRY,
AFRICAN MARIGOLD

17

-

A BUNCH OF WILD ASPARAGUS

26

-

SMOKED HADDOCK
CUSHION

42

-

FIG, TARRAGON

-

I hope — and it really means a lot to me — that the people who work at *La Grenouillère* truly enjoy their time here, both personally and professionally. However, the staff is constantly changing, and this problem is not always easy to manage. Some progress and leave to advance their careers, which seems quite normal to me. Others start here a few months to enrich their CV, as that's how the world of cuisine works. Today, *La Grenouillère* is a place that has an impact on a chef's career. Not so long ago, chefs toured France during their training period. Today, they travel around the world! I don't know how these young people will consolidate all these experiences. This means that I get to work with very cosmopolitan teams that have a lot to offer, but it makes it quite difficult to establish things long term. The question of loyalty sometimes arises. We live in a very guilt-ridden society that is constantly driving people to prove and expand on their experiences. However, loyalty to a recognized chef is also a way in which a trainee chef can gradually find their own style. It's possible to progress simply by reading books! **Physically moving jobs is not the only way to do the world tour. I don't believe that all this moving about is conducive to real professional development.** I sometimes feel that some people come here to work for what they can get rather than really giving anything. I'm considering how we can encourage more loyalty, because the people — and there have been many of them — who stay more than a year, have a lasting impact on the restaurant.

The service must not remain stuck in the past. Nothing should be taken for granted; we need to constantly re-examine all aspects of the restaurant and the changing behaviour and tastes of the guests. It's a fact, for example, that photographs of places or dishes of all restaurants are circulating on social networks today. The dishes I offer rely on an element of surprise and the unexpected. To see them before you come to the restaurant reduces the pleasure of discovery. So, I suggest that during the meal, guests disconnect from their smartphones so that they can more fully enjoy their time here. Certainly, the restaurant is a place that is part of an era but, even if everything evolves, the symbol of the meal table as a place that brings people together to share remains fundamental. We can take photos, obviously. But what remains of the moment? A digital print? The sensory memory seems to me more important. It's also simply a matter of propriety: making calls during mealtimes or answering the phone when eating has always been rude. And the problem has only worsened with mobile phones. One of the primary goals of *La Grenouillère* is that people reconnect with each other and with themselves. It's deplorable — though rare here, fortunately — to see tables where everyone is so absorbed with their smartphone that they no longer see each other. The devices also prevent people from focusing. For my part, I have deactivated the vibrate and notification functions on my phone, which constantly demand attention and distract from the present moment. Obviously, I have nothing against smartphones or social networks per se: they are great tools when we don't allow them to take over. I dream of a world in which the emotions and the senses once again play a central role in our lives. I would like us to become more spontaneous, to rediscover simple pleasures, forgotten gestures and the time we've lost, so that we can find ourselves and enjoy the company of others around a meal or a product. I would like to ensure that we don't disconnect from the real world. And I'm committed to sharing these convictions with my teams.

37

-

YELLOW COURGETTE PAPER

93
-
RED KURI SQUASH,
SMOKED HADDOCK

118
-
TOMATO,
POWDERED PIG

48

-

SUMMER TRUFFLE PANCAKE

119

-

JERUSALEM ARTICHOKE IN A SUGARED ALMOND CRUST

36
-
RAZOR CLAM,
SAND FISH

33
-
MARROW, ROOIBOS

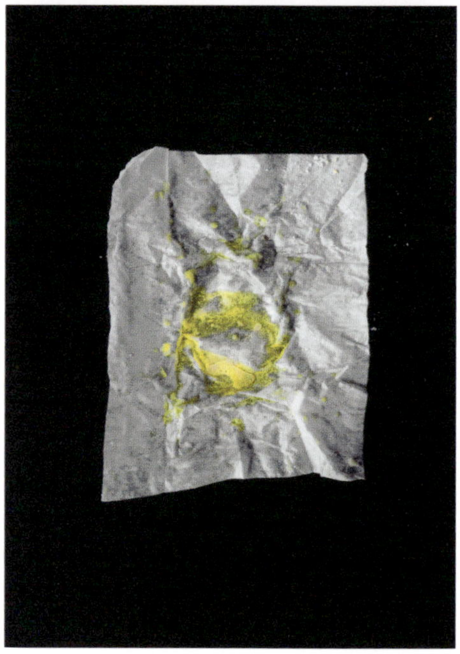

77

-

ABALONE
IN A CRUST

110

-

HERB STALK
SOUFFLÉ

The garden is a key feature of *La Grenouillère*. It invites both contemplation and activity. It's an enclosed space, but it opens out naturally to the surrounding landscape. This seems the right time to mention this setting, which embodies the whole ethos of *La Grenouillère*. We have an extraordinary view of the ramparts of Montreuil-sur-Mer, at the foot of which our restaurant is nestled. The splendid landscape that surrounds us requires that we live up to it! Day after day, the constantly changing light invents infinite shades of green, fresh fluctuations of the apple trees, ever-new skies. When we created the garden, with landscape architect Tiphaine Hameau, we wanted it to be both designed and free. The plots are irregular, the plants seem almost wild, but the straw circles and the rush paths show that it is an appointed space rather than a tamed one. We invite guests to spend time under the apple trees, sitting on stumps, in an orchard that looks like a natural clearing. As Marco Martella — poet, essayist and founder of the journal Jardins, who we have been lucky enough to host here — explains, **we need gardens now more than ever. They allow us to be at one with nature and show us — who are often cut off from the earth — the way back to what's important.** Vast open surfaces dominate in the huts and in the restaurant's dining room and breakfast room: the garden, and more broadly the surrounding landscape, are omnipresent, visible from everywhere, returning us back to nature.

Like the whole house, of which it is an integral part, the garden needs to be constantly evolving, and we continue to modify it, making little changes that add to its personality. We take care of it like a living being that is growing up and whose character is asserting itself. One of the key moments of a meal at *La Grenouillère* is the one where guests taste a honeycomb, notably one from OIivier Darné and Robert Théry's hives. The honeycomb is first presented whole to the customer, then we remove a piece in front of them, with the honey and the wax, which we place on a spoon, adding three drops of lemon juice. Guests let the honey melt in their mouth, then deposit the wax back into the spoon. I'm inspired by an ancestral confectionery that my grandparents used in the countryside to transition between savoury and sweet. Guests can now taste this honey while contemplating the bees flying around the hives that I've set up in the garden. There's a symmetry between the inside and the outside; there's a link between what you're eating and what you're seeing and hearing.

The garden has also been enhanced by the work of wicker producers and weavers Karen Gossart and Corentin Laval, whose work I discovered in the magazine Atelier d'Art. I first invited them to get to know us, then, the magic having worked its effect, proposed that they 'grow' their creations in situ during a three-day residence at *La Grenouillère*. From the breakfast basket to the large, rounded structures in the garden, their wickerwork has found its way into all areas, weaving a harmony between exterior and interior, nature and human creation, art and craftsmanship.

The garden continues to evolve. The ceramicist Lana Ruellan positioned ten of her stardust collectors according to the sky chart on 12 August 2018 at 5.12pm, the date and time when the most shooting stars were travelling through our sky. The idea arose from the fact that tiny particles of stars are continually falling on our heads. Actually, we often forget that shooting stars are meteorites that become powder and light when they enter the atmosphere. These very light microparticles remain in suspension but are precipitated to Earth when it rains, and can thus be collected in the stardust collectors, which filter the rain water. In 2020, the ceramicist will collect this singular rock dust to make a glazed ceramic of a unique colour, in which I will present a dish. We also gave thirty-four small collectors to friends, who were invited to set them up at home and bring us what they collected, creating a sort of *La Grenouillère* galaxy. I find the idea very poetic: it provides such a clear reminder of the fact that we are permanently connected to the universe and that it's a grand thing to be a human being, but also a responsibility. This reversal of scale brings us back to the vanity of our condition: this star dust, which seems infinitely smaller than us, proves to be less insignificant than our time on Earth.

I also wanted to reposition *La Grenouillère* in the garden by bringing it closer to the bridge and the Canche river that explain its original location as the ferryman's house. The place is very popular with walkers and hikers and I also wanted to invite them to come and meet us. So, I created a small herb garden in the form of a maze of wooden boxes planted with aromatic herbs. The herbs are obviously not simply decorative. They are used to create herbal teas to be served at the end of the meal, and can also be used to make bisques, consommés and clear bouillons. But while these herbs inspire the cuisine, that's not their primary role. The idea is also that passers-by put their hands into them and come and talk to us. The marsh lamps by sculptor Laurent Cadilhac stop walkers in their tracks and the benches invite them to sit down and take time to discover the herbs, to contemplate the Canche or to listen to the storyteller of the swamps. This invitation to walkers seems to me a beautiful way to create a natural link between *La Grenouillère* and Madelaine-sous-Montreuil, Montreuil-sur-Mer, the Canche Valley ... For me, it's about creating an open world that blends discreetly but cogently into a site that is itself exceptional and that is part of our common heritage.

105

-

RHUBARB, BIRCH

106
-
RHUBARB,
BINDWEED

92
-
GREEN APPLE,
LANGOUSTINE

07

-

ASPARAGUS TIP TEMPURA

62
-
NETTLE LIQUEUR

111
-
ICED NETTLE SOUFFLÉ

115
-
WOOD SORREL STALKS,
CAPERS

107
-
VEAL SWEETBREAD
IN GREEN SAUCE

06

-

WHITE ASPARAGUS,
BLOOD ORANGE

44

-

COURGETTE FLOWER,
SPIDER CRAB

Maylis de Kerangal wrote a little book, *Un chemin de tables*, in which she recounts the career path of a chef, Mauro, who experiences all the stages of a young chef, from bistrot to gourmet restaurant, in order to create and share his cuisine. He ends up quitting, totally worn out physically and emotionally by the sacrifices the job demands. Although this character is imaginary, the story portrays well what life can be like in the restaurant world on the other side of the kitchen door. It reveals the realities of the tough life of a chef, with its onerous hours, the pressure of high-level catering, carrots to peel every morning, the need to be consistent dish after dish, service after service, day after day. The profession is now very high profile with celebrity chefs and reality shows giving the impression that anyone can realize their dream to become a chef, but they mask the harshness of the job. All this comes at a price. **Cooking takes everything — like a wonderful priesthood.** I'm fortunate enough to be able to thrive in a profession that I've chosen and to enjoy some recognition for what I do, but still. It involves **a life on the fringes**, whether socially or emotionally. I miss out on a lot of things.

Helping my father at the age of twenty-three, I certainly understood what I didn't want to do. If the job is going to cost you everything, you at least need to do it in a way that makes sense to you. If all you experience are daily constraints and toil, the life it involves is simply not worth it. I understand that nothing is ever certain in this profession. I could lose everything tomorrow, but I'm a believer and that gives me hope: I'm hopeful for myself, hopeful for others, hopeful for tomorrow. I firmly believe that tomorrow will be better and that we always reach our goals in the end, provided we do what's needed to get there.

Jacques Brel used to say that true freedom is having the right to get it wrong. I need to continue to take risks. I can't bear the scrutiny of those who judge without ever doing anything and yet are quick to criticize and make remarks. I understand that it's difficult to forgive a chef for a failed dish. I'm on show: my dishes and my cuisine are commented on every day on social networks and elsewhere. But I can't afford to limit myself for fear of getting it wrong. Failure helps you progress. We need to be tolerant of those who try, stumble and get up again. I don't want to settle for the status quo, even if it's working: I have to keep moving forward to stay alive. More than anything else, I fear routine, the signature dish that's so well mastered that it's dead.

Since I arrived at *La Grenouillère*, I've been obsessed with the idea of time passing. I know it's not enough to be good for five or even ten years to make a career. The true appraisal only happens at the end of the road. How many chefs stay their course over the years? How many chefs have not experienced major blows, given up or simply surrendered their convictions to please the clientele? How long can you go on being happy with your cooking, feeling you're being true to yourself, expressing yourself in it? There's a real danger of sticking to what you know, a risk that the path you're taking will become a highway that, while it may interest a certain clientele who want to eat good, gourmet, satisfying food, no longer justifies staying in a job that devours everything.

I wonder how we leave this profession, how we can move forward with equanimity. The career lifespan of a chef is probably comparable to that of a top athlete. Unlike an artist, a chef leaves nothing tangible. This raises the question of legacy: what can we pass on? To whom? And when? I don't have an answer, but **I have seen so few restaurants manage this successfully that it's something I think about every day.**

45

-

WARM STRAWBERRY,
LEMON THYME

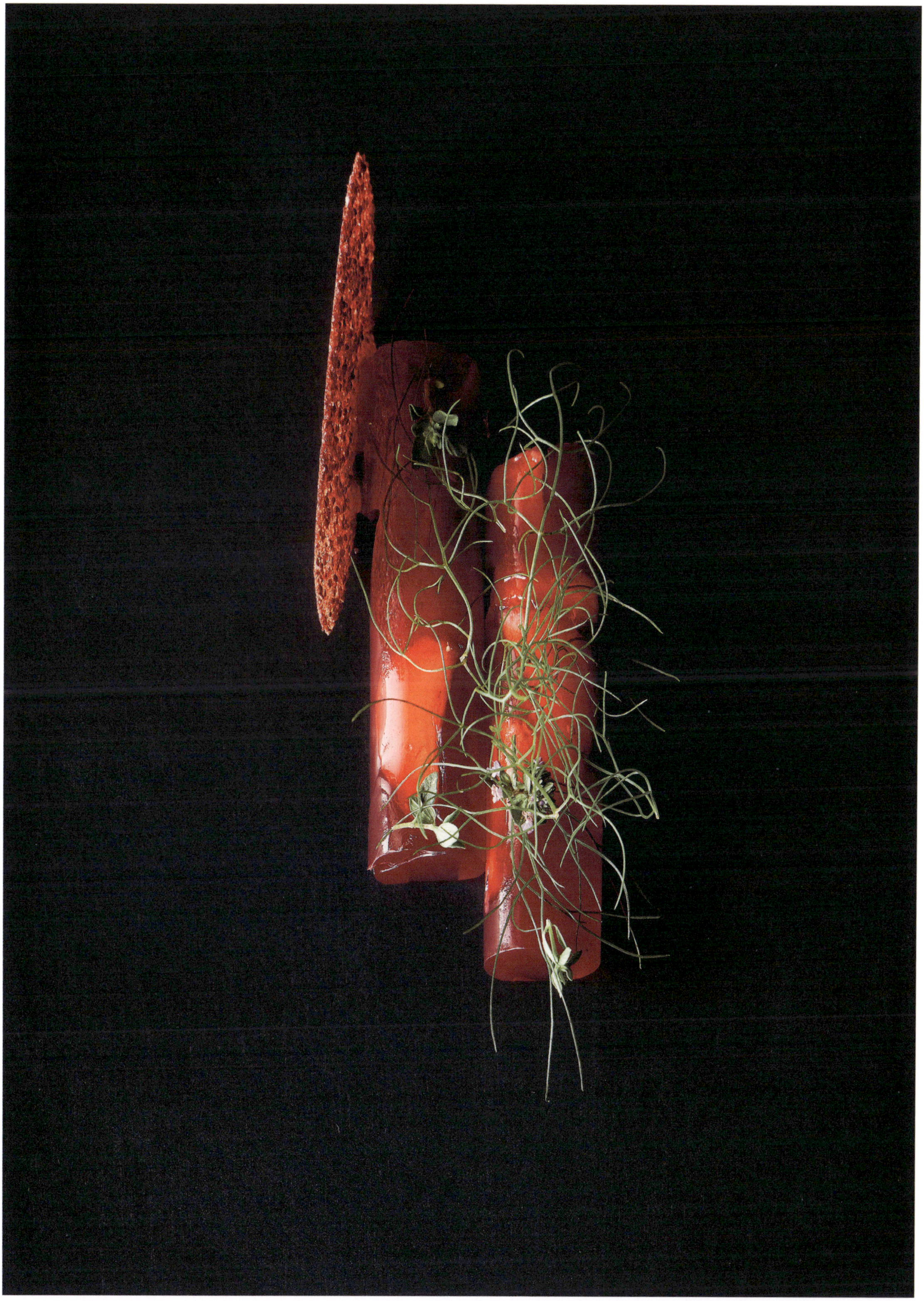

88

-

BEE POLLEN,
CITRON

65

-

HONEYDEW MELON,
LANGOUSTINE

69
-
FROZEN MUSTARD,
PRUNES

56
-
GRASS HERBS 02

114
-
CHICKEN,
LEMON VERBENA

90
-
POTATO,
PRALINÉ

80

-

BURNT PEACH

-

A night at *La Grenouillère*, filled with *anima*

Ryoko Sekiguchi

To dine at Alexandre Gauthier's restaurant is to encounter *anima*. Because that's what defines his cuisine: souls coming to life. There is a particular ecosystem here, unique to the surroundings. Who are the inhabitants of this wonderland? Here is a succinct introduction to the beings that live here.

1. Those that are two while being one – When two sharply acidic drops of vinegar come into contact with the palate, the underside of the tongue perceives all the softness of fluffy potato balls. At another moment, it's the tartness of fava beans that caresses our taste buds while a lobster jumps mischievously against the roof of the mouth. Two textures, two flavours materialize before us, while forming a single entity, like a world split at the horizon. It is our dream, those of us who aspire to be plural. We are presented with a way of life that is different from our own.

2. Those that are the shadow of a presence – What is at the core of a being? The body? The heart? The soul? In this land inhabited by delicious beings, taste is not the only unit of value. Each individual has merit by their presence here. The spider crab makes us aware of the water where once it frolicked, the bud of crystallized tarragon that opens the evening evokes the metallic memory of the first time it broke out of its full-bodied stem. Of course, that relates to its taste, but it also goes beyond taste. Sometimes they evoke the shadow of a presence. Marshmallow, which we can rightly term 'bland', erases saltiness, just as water dripping on a canvas washes the pigments, the trace of its passage creating another painting. The meat of a razor clam, accompanied by egg white and sweetcorn, withdraws, as though to conceal itself beneath this protective veil of mother-of-pearl. The body steps aside, the shadow remains on the ground. We greet it.

3. Those that are asexual – Like angels, the beings that populate this country seem, for the most part, devoid of sex. They would reproduce like jellyfish, driven only by an incessant movement towards life. Tracing clear lines on the plates, multiplied like the structure of a cocoa bean, they dart innocently about as they journey down our throat.

4. Those that long to resemble others – Given the universal desire to have a body other than one's own, we should not be surprised to find this longing elsewhere. What is expressed here is less the achievement of such a transformation as an unfulfilled desire. The langoustine wishes to gain a little of the height of the turnip beside it; the shallots once dreamt of being crystalline creatures, while the meringue disguises itself as a piece of futuristic furniture. The apple would like to clothe itself in the toad's leather, while the salt aspires to the impossible: to be transformed into stardust that would vanish in contact with the tongue. This is when we realize that, in the normal way of things, the desires of these beings go unheard. If we will but give heed to their confessions, all sorts of faces will make their appearance.

5. Those that are green – Sometimes, it seems that the world is organized not according to the kingdoms of nature, but by colour. Whatever is green, grey or white, regardless of its character. Chlorophyll oil is one example. It is not a plant; it is a green element. Just as the flesh of an apple coloured with herbs or a spinach pie assert their presence in the world under the 'green' banner.

6. Those that are spherical – An oval disc, fresh and flat, slips onto the tongue. But not of the sort used by a doctor. No, this is a ceramic 'wafer' from which ones licks a pearl of cow's milk and sturgeon eggs. Welcome to the spherical world. Small living pearls are stirring. Spherical beings are omnipresent here. Blinis and ravioli are spiritual foods. The person who folds their secret into the dough and rolls these ductile little balls in their hands creates an embryo, a new life to be born. They are secretly hoping to see the truth discovered in the eyes of the one who cuts into them. Or who puts them in their mouth, touching them with their palate, their inner hand. The immaculate white ball, the size of a marble, then unfurls its wings. The little lives of the caper flower burst between

Adventure
What will probably happen to someone during the course of their life; probable succession of generally unpredictable events.

Mystery
That in nature or in human destinies which cannot be explained by the human mind; that which is unknowable.

Metamorphosis
The continuous and progressive modification of a shape or light.

Animated
That has life, that has movement.

the teeth. In Japanese, 'to be like a sphere' means to be perfect. It is the world in itself. There is also 'inner' philosophy here. These are foods for mystics, who are drawn to what is hidden away inside a body. Like the whelks taking refuge in a courgette flower. Or the sea bream flesh embedded in cherry tomatoes, alongside other spheres – salmon roe and white currants – like so many eyes watching over us. They are not there to teach life lessons, but they tell us to accept the fact that the world is not made up of foregone conclusions so that we can allow the most beautiful thing to emerge: mystery.

Symbiosis
The close and harmonious association between people or groups of people.

7. Those that grow – The conical shape is characteristic of this place; conical, not phallic. These are beings who by definition resist gravity and aspire to growth. The Tower of Babel, but without its human arrogance. Mushrooms grow at the speed of light; we have all seen it for ourselves in fast-motion films of plant growth. It's a world in which the temporality of living beings is malleable. They blossom so quickly that they become almost diaphanous, as though they were freeing themselves from their bodies. Or like the bacteria that we see busily multiplying behind a microscope. Crystalline, supple, the surprising activity of these particles seems joyful. We watch such phenomena wide-eyed, like a little boy for whom everything is 'the first time in his life'. The world is wide open to him. Things keep on growing, over and over.

Rising
That increases in intensity, in quality; the stem of a plant that takes an upward direction.

8. Those that live in a horizontal world – Here, the animal kingdom, the vegetable kingdom and the bird kingdom are all on the same level. They coexist. Courgettes and zander are in the same world because they were introduced to fire and have been marked by it. A piece of quail, stuffed with sweetbreads, is contrasted with a tansy leaf. Far from being a simple side, the leaf leads us at a brisk pace through the forests, while the caramelized apricot makes us look up at the treetops. A little further on, that underground inhabitant the truffle brings us humus aromas. Our eyes take in several strata: under the earth, on the surface of the earth, above the earth, where plants pour out their souls that are their oils. There is no hierarchy between them: sometimes they exist in close cohabitation, at others, they remain on each other's doorstep, as a sign of mutual respect. Mushrooms, fruits, birds and herbs live in harmony in the same world, and a dish can be a witness to this fact.

Wonder
An event or thing that causes great astonishment because of its strange and extraordinary character.

Of course, all these beings were born in this land, but that's not the main message. It doesn't matter where they were born or the climate they lived in before they met us. What matters is that they were actually alive. And that, having passed through this kitchen, they have acquired a different sort of life. These new individuals, like paleontological creatures, are unknown to us although they are inhabitants of the same Earth. Being completely independent and free, it is possible that they may not understand our language. But that is what makes them so enchanting as they gaze at us with all their spherical 'eyes'. We look at them. Small worlds. Then we invite them to come inside us. How is our life transformed by digesting these wonderful strangers? We don't yet know.

Those that lived with us and accompanied us on our visit of this land: Tarragon, Anchovy, Cucumber, Fish entrails, Potato, Vinegar, Forget-Me-Not, Shallot, Mimolette, Cow's Milk, Sturgeon Eggs, Turnip, Capsule, Langoustine, Yarrow, Razor Shell, Sweetcorn, Egg White, Meadowsweet, Geranium, Sea Bass, Crab, Stilton, Weever, Plankton, Walnut, Olive, Zander, Courgette, Pollen, Mangetout, Peppered Mackerel, Nasturtium, Roast Chicken, Caper, Spider Crab, Quail, Apricot, Sweetbreads, Tansy, Truffle, Wild Chervil, Honey, Goats' Milk, 'Mara des Bois' Strawberry, Apple, Wild Strawberry, Verbena, Mint, Rocket, Elderberry, Cherry Tomato, Sea Bream, Pansy, Courgette Flower, Spinach, Broad Bean, Watermelon, Basil, Pepper, Chlorophyll, Tomato, Rapeseed, Peach, Grapefruit, Broccoli, Fennel, Lemon Balm, Sorrel, Cacao, Gooseberry, White Currant, Frog.

-

Alexandre Gauthier, cook from the edge

Laurent Seminel

How can we describe a man's cuisine? How can we explain its complexity without simplifying it? Present its singularity without distorting it? Alexandre Gauthier's cuisine adheres to no particular style, but it does have an allure. And that is something completely different. A style can be copied; an allure attracts attention. It is an identity. The cuisine at *Anecdote* also has an allure, although its style is very different from that of *La Grenouillère*. Both form part of Alexandre Gauthier's culinary identity.

Gauthier has no complexes but he does have questions, no culinary preconceptions but lots of thoughts, no limitations but a territory. He is a man living on the edge, in that imperceptible but precise place where the forest ends and the glade begins. His cuisine is also on the edge, at the place where classicism and avant-garde intersect. It is obviously creative, but to describe it as such is simplistic; it is essentially classic, but that term is insufficient to do it justice.

A man of the marshland, Gauthier is also on the border between land and water. He has not forgotten that Montreuil was once a port. In all its complexity, *La Grenouillère* is a coastal restaurant. The sea may have receded, but it has left some dishes in its wake. Alexandre's cuisine is an incessant ebb and flo, where the classic engulfs the modern or the modern consumes the classic. The lines become blurred, submerged by a cuisine which, for all that, remains very clear. So it is with Alexandre Gauthier's cuisine, which is more classic than it seems at first glance yet is contemporary to the last bite.

As Giuseppe Tomasi di Lampedusa wrote in his novel *The Leopard*, 'If we want things to stay as they are, things will have to change'. In the speech he made while making Alexandre Gauthier an *Officier des Arts et Lettres*, Jack Lang recalled in detail two of Alexandre's dishes that he had enjoyed 15 years previously. Cooking is an ephemeral art that sometimes leaves indelible traces. Arts and letters: two words that fit Alexandre well. The opportunity he gave George Rousse to create installations in a delapidated building is enlightening on this subject. This was not the whim of a patron, but the mirror of his own work. George Rousse's art is ephemeral like Alexandre's cooking. And they both require a certain perspective to be perceived, an effort to be understood. In his horizontal landscape, Alexandre Gauthier invents mountains to move. He is a man who likes a challenge. In the soft soil of the marshes, he never stops building. He redevelops and renovates huts here, baths there.

While today *La Grenouillère* is part of Les Grandes Tables du Monde, Relais & Châteaux and among the few two-Michelin-starred restaurants, it has nevertheless retained a certain rebellious streak. Alexandre is a free man who is constantly appearing where we least expect him. In a world of gastronomy where luxury is omnipresent, where rare ingredients have become ordinary, he highlights simple products and a humble and everyday cuisine. It is culinary Arte Povera.

Alexandre has defined his territory, established his rules, imposed his vision. His cooking is challenging to produce and challenging to understand. To do so, you need to go beyond questioning and ignore the surprise elicited by certain dishes. Cuisine is not a gadget or an accessory for cooks lacking creativity. It's a speech, a novel, where you have to learn the language, read between the lines and notice the silences. Each dish is a sentence, whose meaning needs to be understood. But this meaning can only be grasped if we know the preceding sentence and the dishes that follow it. Cuisine is an art of remembrance; it pays tribute and overthrows, it revolutionizes and enthrones.

La Grenouillère is a unique place, a culmination. Dining here is both a jubilation and a lesson. It is the proof, at each visit, of the chasm that separates Alexandre Gauthier from his peers. It is not a question of talent or techniques, but rather a question of vision. Sometimes one person's work can shake up a profession. In art, there is a before and after Marcel Duchamp; in cuisine, there will surely be a before and after Alexandre Gauthier.

-

THE TEAM

Émilie
Florence
Isabelle

Camille
Elise
Junya

Adrien
Léa
Romain

Virginie
Fanny
Nathalie

Prisca
Laura
Déborah

Leigh-Anne
Charlotte
Émeline

Nidta
Jérémy
Soizic

Julien
Rodolphe
François

Mickaël
Mathilde
Kohei

Quentin
Noémie
Simon

Chun-Hao
Noémie
Sébastien

Charlotte
Ousmane
Margaux

Valentin
Farès
Éric

Jessica
Valérie
Timothée

Rudy
Yann
Clara

Éva
Gwenaelle
David

Emmanuel
Samuel
Alexandre, Eustache, Roland

Félix
Jérôme

Alix
Toshiharu

Lizzie
Yuki

-

THE RECIPES

The recipes in this book generally serve eight. They have been designed to be created in a restaurant kitchen. This book has been designed to present my cuisine as I apply and serve it in my restaurant La Grenouillère.

01 / P. 214

Burnt apricot, marjoram

The genius of the apricot is contained in its kernel.

10 large, ripe apricots (rouge du Roussillon variety), 300 g sugar, 1,5 litre spring water, 1 bunch marjoram, 200 g apricot kernel oil, 2 g yellow pectin.

Make a syrup by boiling 200 g sugar with the spring water and half of the marjoram. Wash the apricots, boil them gently in the syrup for 2 minutes, then cover with cling film and let sit for 6 hours. Halve and stone the apricots, peel them gently. Return the skins to the syrup, laying them flat and making sure they're immersed to avoid oxidation. Also set aside 10 poached half-apricots in the syrup and use the other apricots to make a jammy compote — drain 250 g of them, heat them in a saucepan ; add the yellow pectin and 100 g sugar. Cook until thick and sticky. Blend with a hand mixer, and rub through a sieve. Spoon into a piping bag. Pick out about twenty marjoram tops and blend the rest of the bunch with the apricot kernel oil. Strain through a sieve and pour into a squeeze bottle. To serve, start by placing the apricot skins on the plates, then burn them with a blow torch. Cut the apricot halves in two, and put two pieces into apricot skins. Fill an apricot skin with the apricot compote, and another skin with the marjoram oil. Decorate with marjoram tops.

02 / P. 23

Vegetable sea anemone

The cool taste of lemon verbena, a burnt taste of the sea as a seasoning. A flaky vegetable texture reminiscent of seaweed.

5 yellow courgettes, 50 g sea lettuce, 50 cl spring water, 1 lemon, 10 g nori seaweed, 3,5 g Iota, 50 cl milk, 2 g Sucro, 2 bunches lemon verbena, 200 g peanut oil, fine salt.

One day ahead, make the sea water: combine the spring water, 20 g sea lettuce, the nori and 1/4 of the lemon in a sous-vide bag. Seal the bag and refrigerate overnight. The next day, strain the contents of the bag, stir the Iota into the water and bring to a boil. Let cool. Pluck out the verbena leaves from the stalks, and set aside a few tops. Toast the remaining 30 g of sea lettuce on a plancha and blend it with the peanut oil. Bring the milk to a boil, add the lemon verbena leaves, cover the saucepan with cling film and let sit for 30 minutes. Strain, then blend with the Sucro with a hand mixer. Season with salt. Trim the yellow courgettes and laminate them into large sheets with a Japanese turning slicer. Roll the sheets into tight cylinders, 3 to 4 cm in diameter. Tie them with string and steam for 2 to 3 minutes. Cut them into slanted lengths, pour some seaweed oil onto the plates and stand the courgette rolls upright on the oil. Alongside the rolls, place a spoonful of jellied sea water, a few verbena tops, and serve with a small bowl of lemon verbena emulsion on the side.

03 / P. 155

Smoked eel

The taste of the marshes, of the lake, of all these weeds that surround them, with the smell of a campfire added to it.

2 kg smoked eel, 2 kg spinach, 40 cl white balsamic condiment, 50 cl distilled water, 2,5 g Algin, 6,5 cl spring water, 16 g glucose, 14,5 g sugar, 4,5 g xanthan gum, marsh herbs (common yarrow, wood worrel, arugula, herb Robert, sweet cicely).

In a large saucepan, cover 500 g smoked eel (skin on and bones in) with 1 litre water. Simmer, without boiling, for 20 minutes, strain, and boil down by two thirds. Set aside. Skin the remaining smoked eel and shred the meat between your fingers, avoiding any bone, to make eel rillettes. Parboil the spinach in plenty of boiling water for 1 minutes, cool them immediately in iced water, squeeze excess water and puree in a Thermomix until smooth. Add the eel stock, pour into a piece of cloth and let it drip through until you can collect a smooth puree from the cloth. Spoon it into a piping bag fitted with a smooth nozzle. Make some white balsamic droplets : blend the Algin with the distilled water. In another container, blend the white balsamic condiment, sugar, xanthan gum, glucose, and spring water. Using an inversed spherification kit, add the vinegar mix drop by drop to the Algin bath. Leave to set, drain and rinse. Clean the herbs, keeping only the tender young sprigs. To serve, use a round cutter to place some eel rillettes onto each plate. Cover with smoked spinach puree. Add 1 teaspoonful of white balsamic condiment, and cover with marsh herbs in a harmonious pattern.

04 / P. 28
-

Crispy artichoke, chamomile

Artichoke and chamomile, their subtlety combined to a slightly sour, potent fresh goat cheese.

25 artichokes, 5 small poivrade artichokes, 150 g spinach puree, 400 g flour, 62,5 g egg yolks, 150 g fresh goat cheese, 25 g dry goat cheese, 1 lemon, 10 cl lemon-scented oil, 10 cl olive oil, oil for deep-frying, chamomile.

Turn 24 artichokes and cook them sous-vide with the oils at 100 °C/212 °F for 25 minutes. Let cool, drain, and blend until smooth. Rub through a sieve and keep in a piping bag. Turn the last artichoke, slice it finely with a mandolin, then cut it in fine julienne strips. Immediately deep-fry them in 130 °C/270 °F oil for 4 to 5 minutes, until golden and crispy. Drain on kitchen paper and keep in a dry place. Turn the poivrade artichokes, setting aside the hearts and some of the leaves. Cut the hearts in two, and store them in a sous-vide bag, vacuumed with a little lemon juice and olive oil. Make a raviole dough : in a stand mixer fitted with the hook implement, mix the flour, egg yolks and spinach puree for 8 minutes at speed 1. Then put this dough in a sous-vide bag and vacuum. Mix the fresh goat cheese and the finely grated dry goat cheese and spoon them into a piping bag. Roll out the raviole dough at the finest setting. Cut out 5 x 3 cm strips. Onto the middle of each strip, drop a teaspoonful of artichoke puree. Moisten the edges of the dough, fold over and seal. Make a second batch of ravioles and fill them with the cheese stuffing in the same manner. To serve, draw two lines of artichoke puree on the plates. Sear the ravioles in a hot oiled frying pan on both sides, and place them on the puree. Add the poivrade artichoke salad and some chamomile leaves.

05 / P. 143
-

White asparagus, fermented turnip broth

The bud's acidity is balanced by that of the lactofermented turnip.

4 quince, 16 turnips, 1 litre water, 20 g salt, 8 asparagus, 1 lemon, common yarrow, 400 g butter, 20 g green oil, olive oil.

The turnips should be left to ferment at least three weeks before you start. Sterilize a Le Parfait or Mason jar in a 100 °C/212 °F steam oven for 10 minutes. Mix the salt and water. Peel and quarter the turnips, put them in the jar, pour the salted water over them. Close the jar and leave it for 3 days in a warm place, making sure you open it once everyday. After three days, tightly close the jar for 3 weeks and refrigerate at 3 °C/37.4°F. Ferment the quince according to the exact same method. Wrap the lemon in foil and bake it for 8 to 12 hours in a 170 °C/340 °F oven. Keep in a dry place. Peel the asparagus and keep 5 cm of the tips. Cut the remaining parts into 2-mm slices. Reconstruct each asparagus and wrap it in a damp cloth. Pluck out the leaves from the yarrow and discard the stalks. Make a green oil according to the instructions for the crunchy peas. On low heat, melt 500 g butter in 50 cl of the turnips' fermenting juice, then emulsify with a hand blender and season with salt. Bake the reconstructed asparagus with a little olive oil for 2 minutes in a 170 °C/340 °F oven. Burn them on all sides with a blow torch. Season with salt, transfer each asparagus to a bowl, and cover with two chunks of fermented quince. Lavisly grate some burnt lemon over the bowls in order to cover the composition. Add a drop of green oil and yarrow leaves. Pour 2 cl of the turnip broth into each bowl.

06 / P. 254
-

White asparagus, blood orange

Fresh and juicy like a seasonal salad.

20 white asparagus (28/32 to a kilo), 10 blood oranges, 1 mozzarella, 1 bunch red mustard, fleur de sel, olive oil, 4 g xanthan gum.

Peel the oranges, cut out their segments and bake them for 8 minutes in a 170 °C / 340 °F oven. Squeeze the remaining oranges and blend their juice with the xanthan gum. Pour into a piping bag. Store the mozzarella in a deep-freezer. Peel the asparagus and slice them 1-mm thick lengthwise with a mandolin cutter. Roll these slices into hollow tubes. Place them side by side on a line on each plate and fill one out of two tubes with the blood orange gel, and the remaining tubes with the baked segments. Season with fleur de sel and olive oil. Decorate each tube with mustard shoots and grate the frozen mozzarella over the plates.

07 / P. 248

Asparagus tip tempura

The wild nettle – the weed with the worst reputation – treated like spinach or a seasoning.

1 kg spinach, 8 white asparagus tips, 900 g tempura batter (see Herb tempura), *oil for deep-frying.*

Cook the spinach for 3 minutes in boiling salted water. Cool them immediately in iced water, then blend them in a Thermomix at speed 10 for 1 minute. Make the tempura batter and divide it into three equal parts : leave one plain. Make a green batter with the second part, coloring it with 100 g spinach puree. Make a tempura foam from the third part : pour it into a siphon, add 2 gas cartridges, then pour it into a container. Parboil the asparagus heads for 5 minutes in a 85 °C/185 °F steam oven. Assemble them three by three, 2 cm apart, on a skewer inserted 2 cm from the bottom of the stalks. Dip 6 cm of the tips in the foamy tempura batter. Position the skewered asparagus on the edges of the deep-fryer in order to fry only the tips, and deep-fry at 170 °C/340 °F for 2 minutes. Drain, dip 4 cm of the tips in the green tempura, and deep-fry again for 2 minutes. Finally, dip 1 cm of the tips into the plain tempura and deep-fry for 2 more minutes. The different colours, temperatures and degrees of cooking should be clearly noticeable.

08 / P. 212

Aubergine, cod liver

Two similar marrow-like textures – the marine silkiness of cod liver enhanced by the burnt aubergine.

6 aubergines, 1 tin high-quality cod liver in oil (by J.-C. David in Boulogne sur Mer), 135 g cream, sunflower oil for deep-frying, fleur de sel, 2 g xanthan gum, organic rapeseed oil, 2 cl milk, olive oil.

Grill 4 aubergines over hot Japanese binchotan coals. When they are scorched and browned all over, remove them from the grill and scoop out the flesh. Immediately cover it with olive oil to avoid oxidation. Dry the skins in a dehydrator, then pulverize them.
Puree 300 g aubergine flesh in a blender with the cream and xanthan gum. Season with salt, spoon into a siphon and add one gas cartridge. Preheat the sunflower oil to 170 °C/340 °F, and cut the two remaining aubergines into 1,5 mm slices on a ham slicer. As you cut them, throw the slices into the hot oil in order to fry them before they discolour. When they're golden brown, lift them out of the oil and drain on kitchen paper. Arrange them on racks and dry them in a 50° C/122 °F dehydrator, fan on. To serve, arrange the pieces of smoked aubergines on the plates.
Place a well-drained chunk of cod liver on top. Cover with a mound of aubergine mousse, and quickly paste the aubergine crisps over the composition, concealing it completely. Season with fleur de sel, burnt aubergine powder, and drizzle with rapeseed oil.

09 / P. 27

Green baba

Take a classic and plant it in herbal territory to change its identity.

250 g all-purpose flour, 1 bunch wild mint, 2 eggs, 1 bunch wild chervil, 25 g inverted sugar, 1 bunch curly dock (wild sorrel), 50 g softened butter, 1 sprig tansy, 165 g sugar, 1 bunch flatleaf parsley, 50 cl spring water, 1 sprig wild celery, 28,5 cl milk, 1/2 lemon, 100 g unwhippd cream, 100 g whipped cream, 1 bunch common yarrow, 2 sheets gelatin, 80 g egg yolks, 500 g spinach, 5 g fine salt.

Make the herb granita: combine the leaves of 10 g mint, 40 g curly dock, 40 g parsley and a few leaves of wild celery with 40 g cream in a deep-freezer. Once hardened, blend immediately into a granita, and freeze.
Store in deep-freezer. Wash and drain the spinach, run them through a juice extractor. Make the baba dough: in a stand mixer fitted with the hook implement, combine the flour, eggs, inverted sugar, salt and 15 cl spinach juice. Beat at speed 3 for 10 minutes, add the butter, and knead until the dough separates from the bowl. Leave to rise for 2 hours in a cool place. Grease some baba moulds, 4,5 cm in diameter, and drop 20 g of the dough into each mould. Let sit until the dough starts to rise above the rims. Bake in a 180 °C / 350 °F oven for 10 minutes. Unmould just out of the oven, and let cool for 3 to 4 hours.
Make a crème anglaise: soak the gelatin in cold water. Boil the milk and cream. Whisk the egg yolks and 40 g sugar until pale and creamy. Whisk in the milk and cream gradually, and cook, stirring, until the custard thickens. Off the heat, dissolve the drained gelatin in the custard, and refrigerate until set.
Using a hand mixer, blend this Bavarian cream with 20 g curly dock leaves, a few wild celery leaves, 25 g parsley and 5 g mint. Strain through a sieve, and fold in the whipped cream. Pour into a piping bag. Bring the spring water to a boil with 125 g sugar. Let cool,

then blend with the lemon juice, the tansy, 25 g curly dock leaves, a few mint leaves and a few celery leaves. Rub through a fine sieve and keep refrigerated. Cut each baba in two, soak them in the green syrup. Drain.
Make a quenelle of herb cream on the edge of a plate, cover it with the soaked baba, add a few yarrow leaves and, on the side, the herb granita. Serve the chilled syrup on the side, in a sauce boat.

10 / P. 165

-

Knife-cut sea bass, flowers

Pick, fish, trim. The happiness of simple gestures.

1 200-g fillet of sea bass olive oil, fleur de sel, burnet shoots, chervil shoots, red pimpernel shoots and flowers, red-veined sorrel shoots.

Peel off the skin from the fillet, cut the fillet into small cubes. Add a dash of olive oil, some fleur de sel, and roll into 10-g balls. Just before serving, roll these balls in a mix of young shoots and flowers.

11 / P. 72

-

Sea bass and peas

An interesting mouthfeel, enhanced by the silkiness of sea bass.

5 kg fresh peas, 300 g sea bass fillet, 500 g small pickled onions in vinegar, ascorbic acid, 10 g xanthan gum, 5 cl milk, salt, 3 g B methyl cellulose, 100 g cream, forget-me-nots, olive oil.

Shell the peas (set 100 g aside) and parboil them in a large saucepan of water for 6 minutes. Cool them immediately under cold running water. Run the pea pods through a juicer, and add the ascorbic acid to prevent discolouring. Blend 50 cl of this juice with the xanthan gum, run through a sous-vide machine to eliminate any air bubbles, then pour into a piping bag. Blend 1 kg of cooked peas until smooth, rub through a sieve, and collect 500 g puree. Mix it with the milk, 7 g salt, and the methyl cellulose. Finally, add the cream. Pour into a siphon and add 2 gas cartridges. Peel 100 g fresh peas, season them with salt and olive oil Peel off the skin from the sea bass fillets, dice the flesh. Season them with olive oil and salt. To serve, place a cube of sea bass on the plate, and add a tablespoonful of shelled and seasoned peas. Partially cover the composition with the pea foam from the siphon, and fill the halved onions with pea pod gel. Decorate with sprigs of forget-me-not.

12 / P. 40
-

Snipe, white sugar beet

A bird and a root, both typical of my Montreuil terroir.

1 plait of smoked Arleux garlic, 8 snipe, 2 white sugar beets, 50 cl clear spirit vinegar, 50 cl spring water, 1 bunch herb Robert (wild geranium), olive oil, fine salt, freshly ground black pepper, 150 g clarified butter, 100 g unsalted butter.

Peel the white beets, wash them thoroughly, and cut them into cylinders, 1 cm in diameter. Count 4 or 5 cylinders per serving.
Bring the spirit vinegar to a boil with the water and a little salt. Place the beet cylinders in glass preserving jars and pour the boiling vinegar to the top of the jars. Seal tightly, and let sit for two days. You may use a Gastrovac to hasten the process (1 hour at 50° C/122 °F).
Pluck, singe, and gut the snipe. Stuff their throats with the white beet trimmings.
Brown the snipe in olive oil, then roast them in a 170 °C/340 °F oven for 5 minutes with the plait of smoked garlic. In a sauté pan, brown the beet cylinders with the butter.
Just out of the oven, baste the snipe with a knob of butter mixed with a few mashed smoked garlic cloves. Season with salt. Arrange the white beet cylinders on the plates.
Add the snipe, and dress it in herb Robert leaves. Serve the smoked garlic-infused cooking butter in a sauce boat.

13 / P. 63
-

Comfrey fritters

A wild spinach, with minimal handling.

10 young, tender comfrey leaves, 150 g pastry flour, 200 g iced water, 1 egg yolk, fleur de sel, pepper, 250 g egg whites, 50 g hazelnut oil, 100 g de unsweetened hazelnut paste, 1 bunch comfrey flowers, oil for deep-frying.

Line a rimmed baking sheet with cling film. Pour the egg whites onto this, then cover the sheet with cling film and pierce it in several places with a pick. Cook in a 80 °C/175 °F steam oven for 15 minutes. Let cool, then puree in a blender, adding the hazelnut oil and hazelnut paste. Season with salt, and pour into a piping bag. Make a tempura batter — without overmixing, stir the iced water and egg yolk into the flour. Lightly brush the comfrey leaves with the batter and deep-fry in 170 °C/340 °F oil. Pat dry and season with salt. In the middle of each tempura, pipe a mound of hazelnut cream and cover with the comfrey flowers.

14 / P. 107
-

Mimolette fritters

The delicacy of Northern France's version of Parmesan.

150 g medium-aged mimolette cheese, 25 g egg (half an egg), 125 g tapioca powder, 8 g butter, 3 g fine salt, 10 cl milk, peanut oil.

Blend the mimolette into a paste. Pulverize the tapioca in a blender. Combine all the ingredients in a stand mixer and knead for about 5 minutes, until smooth.
Refrigerate the dough until stiff, and shape it into even-sized balls of 10 g each.
Shortly before serving, deep-fry the balls in 170 °C/340 °F peanut oil for 2 to 3 minutes, and serve immediately.

15 / P. 44

Rusk, pea, broad bean

Crusty, crunchy, crispy.

250 g all-purpose flour, 11,5 cl spring water, 10 g olive oil, 5 g fine salt, 300 g fresh peas, 20 cl milk, 10 fresh young broad beans in their pods, 5 dried apricots, 1 salt-cured lemon, hazelnut oil, 1 bunch mustard greens, 1 bunch pansies.

In a stand mixer fitted with the hook implement, knead the rusk dough with the flour, water, oil, and salt for 5 minutes. Insert the dough into a sous-vide bag and refrigerate for 1 hour. Cook the peas in salted boiling water, cool them in iced water, drain and puree them in a blender with the milk and a little hazelnut oil. Rub through a sieve and spoon into a piping bag. Shell the broad beans and peel every bean. Refrigerate. Finely dice the dried apricots and the salt-cured lemon (discarding the pulp and the white part of the peel). Arrange the rusks on the plates, spread them with the pea puree, scatter the diced apricot and lemon over these, then add the shelled broad beans. Decorate with small mustard leaves and pansy petals.

16 / P. 178

Whole milk blini, crab meat

Luscious texture. The taste of raw milk and butter, the saltiness of crab.

1 litre milk, 17,3 g xanthan gum, 7,5 g salt, 91,67 g rice flour, 250 g egg whites, 400 g fresh crab meat, 350 g butter, 40 cl spring water, 250 g butter, powdered burnt bread (see Black trumpet mushroom and lichen).

Preheat a fan oven to 170 °C/340 °F. Mix the xanthan gum, salt, and rice flour. Heat the milk on low heat, bring to a boil, then pour it over the mixed dry ingredients, blending with a hand mixer. Once the milk is completely incorporated, blend in the egg whites. Keep blending until smooth, then pour into a piping bag. Cut a 15 x 25 cm rectangle of parchment paper and pipe 20 g of batter over it. Cover with a rectangle of parchment paper of the same size and roll out to a thickness of 2 mm. Repeat until there is no batter left. Bake the blinis in their paper on a baking sheet for 5 minutes without stacking them. Turn them over and bake for 4 more minutes. Remove the top sheet of paper and bake for 2 more minutes. The edge of each blini should be colored. In a saucepan, combine 50 g butter, 5 cl water and the crab meat. Cover with a disk of parchment paper, and stew for 5 minutes on low heat. Correct seasoning. To serve, reheat the blinis in a 170 °C/340 °F fan oven, for no more than 1 minute. Sprinkle the plates with burnt bread. Spread 1 tablespoon of crab meat between two blinis, then fold them in two and add this to the plate. Make a beurre noisette emulsion : cook 250 g butter until light brown, then add 35 cl spring water to interrupt cooking. Emulsify with a hand blender, add to the plates, and serve.

17 / P. 220

A bunch of wild asparagus

The foragers's reward, with a few flowers thrown in.

About 20 freshly picked wild asparagus from the sand dunes, 1 bunch forget-me-nots, 1 bunch chives, 200 g pistachios, 50 g fruity olive oil, 3 g Glice, fleur de sel.

Trim the asparagus, removing the lower part of the stalks, then cut the asparagus in two or four lengthwise. Collect the trimmings, run them through a juice extractor.
Blend the pistachios into a smooth puree. Heat the olive oil to 60 °C/140 °F and stir in the Glice. Let cool. Combine this gelified oil and the pistachio puree. Emulsify with a hand mixer, adding the asparagus juice. Season with salt, and refrigerate. Parboil the chives. Collect the asparagus 'pencils' in bunches with the forget-me-nots. Tie them with blanched chives, and serve them in a glass of water. Serve with the pistachio mayonnaise.

18 / P. 90

-

Grilled broccoli, smoked herring droplets

The pairing of almost nothing with almost nothing. A noble taste.

3 heads broccoli, 1 bunch basil, 2 smoked herring fillets, 1 kg spinach 10 g Algin, 24 g Calcic, 1 bunch chervil, 2 bunches flatleaf parsley, 280 g peanut oil, 1 litre spring water, 10 small oysters, salt.

Chop the herring fillets and cover them with the spring water in a saucepan. Simmer gently for 1 hour. Off the heat, cover with cling film and let sit for 1 hour. Strain. Refrigerate, then remove the fat on the surface. Season with salt. Wash the spinach, run through a juice extractor. Measure 50 cl herring broth and stir in 5 g Algin. Vacuum to eliminate all air bubbles. Season the spinach juice with the remaining herring broth. Measure 50 cl of this juice and eliminate air bubbles as above. Stir the Calcic into 1 litre tap water. Using a squeeze bottle, make droplets of alginated herring broth. Wait for the droplets to set, then drain and rinse. Repeat this operation with the spinach broth. Store the droplets in a little pure herring broth. Halve a head of broccoli lengthwise, cook it in boiling salted water. Drain, let cool, and sear each half on one side until browned. Parboil the basil. Puree the broccoli and basil with a little salt and peanut oil. Pick the best florets from the remaining broccoli and cool them *al dente* in boiling salted water. Puree the flatleaf parsley and 250 g peanut oil, rub through a sieve and pour into a squeeze bottle. Halve the cooked broccoli florets, sear them on their cut side on a plancha, then bake. On each plate, drop a spoonful of pureed broccoli. Mix the green and white droplets with the parsley oil and chervil. Shuck the oysters, sear them on one side, and lay them onto the puree. In front, place the hot broccoli and scatter the droplets on the side to hide the oyster. Add a dash of parsley oil.

19 / P. 51

-

Purple Brussels sprout, sugar

The earth as dessert. Discolored cabbage sprout, cream of root vegetable.

30 purple Brussels sprouts, 30 cl lemon juice, 250 Jerusalem artichokes, 200 g milk, 1 vanilla pod, 50 g sugar cane syrup, 1,5 g sheet gelatin, 300 g cream, 5 g icing sugar.

Make the Jerusalem artichoke foam : peel the artichokes and cook them in half milk, half water. When they are tender, add ½ vanilla pod, cover and let sit for 10 minutes. Drain, puree the artichokes in a blender and rub through a sieve. Soak the gelatin in cold water for 10 minutes. To 200 g of artichoke puree, add the drained gelatin. Mix well, then add 100 g cream and the syrup. Pour into a siphon, add 2 gas cartridges. Pour the foam into semi-spherical silicone moulds and deep-freeze them immediately until hard. Pluck out the leaves from the purple Brussels sprouts, parboil them in water, immediately throw them into iced water, then soak them in the lemon juice for at least 2 hours. Beat the remaining cream until stiff with the icing sugar and the seeds from the remaining half of the vanilla pod. Serve on round plates : spread the whipped cream into a disk, add a half-sphere of ice cream, and cover with more whipped cream. Carefully and gracefully cover the dome with cabbage leaves from bottom to top, and serve immediately.

20 / P. 60

-

Bulbous chervil, hazelnut

The subtlety of smoked garlic, the chestnut taste of chervil root.

40 bulbous chervil roots, 2 heads white garlic, 1 head smoked Arleux garlic, 8 cl spring water, 3,6 g Iota, 4,8 g fine salt, 4 g sugar, fleur de sel, 50 g unsalted butter, 100 g blanched hazelnuts, olive oil.

Peel the white garlic, parboil it 4 or 5 times in a row. Grill it in a pan, or on a plancha, and blend it with a little olive oli and salt. Spoon into a piping bag. Quarter the head of smoked garlic, brown it in a dry pan, then add the spring water. Simmer for 10 minutes, then cover the pan with cling film and let sit for 1 hour. Strain, measure 6 cl of this stock and add the Iota, fine salt, and sugar. Bring to a boil and pour into a plastic container. Let cool. Peel the bulbous chervil roots. Halve or quarter them depending on their size. Put them into a sous-vide bag with the butter, and steam for a few minutes. Take them out of the bag and sear them on a plancha with a little olive oil. On the plate, pipe a few dots of grilled garlic puree. Place the chervil roots upright on the garlic puree. Add a spoonful of smoked garlic jelly, and finely grate the hazelnuts over the plate with a Microplane grater.

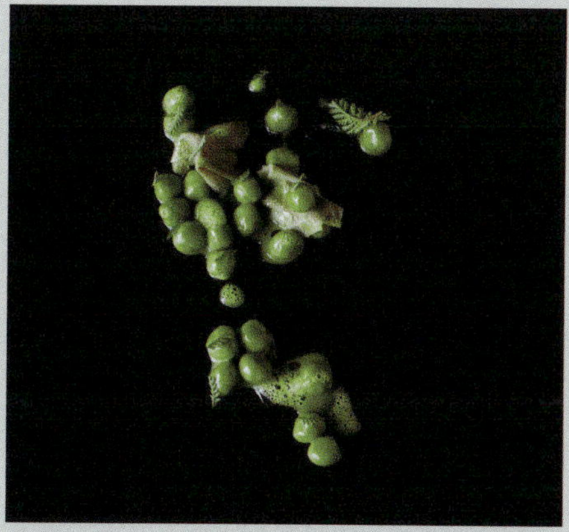

21 / P. 200

Capers, tansy

The meeting of three strong characters.

500 g beef tripe, 1 kg bintje potatoes, 2 bunches flatleaf parsley (leaves only), 40 g Parmesan cheese, 1 egg yolk, 75 g all-purpose flour, 5 g fine salt, 250 g capers, 250 g unsalted butter, 1 bunch tansy, olive oil, fleur de sel, 1 onion studded with a few cloves, 1 carrot, 1 bouquet garni.

Soak the tripe in cold water until clean and white. Cook it in stock for 1 hour and a half with the onion, carrot and bouquet garni. Bake the potatoes in their skins in a 170 °C/340 °F oven for 1 hour, then cut them open and bake them for 15 more minutes. Scoop out the pulp and run it through a food mill. Pat dry the parsley leaves, run them through a juice extractor, and set aside the pulp. Drain the capers and pat them dry. Make the gnocchi dough: in a bowl, combine the egg yolk with the salt and Parmesan cheese. In another bowl, stir half the parsley pulp into 500 g mashed potatoes, and work this gently by hand, without overkneading, then stir in the flour. Shape the dough into olive-sized balls and insert a caper into each one. Roll into small balls with your palms and deep-freeze. Make a whisked butter sauce and, when it is light and creamy, stir in the remaining parsley pulp. Cook the frozen gnocchi in boiling salted water. On a plancha, sear the tripe with a little olive oil. Season with salt and pepper. Toss the gnocchi in the parsley butter with the tripe and 2 sprigs tansy. Arrange these on plates and add a few thin tansy leaves to finish the dish.

22 / P. 217

Purple carrot

Cooking, color, lively architecture – the silkiness of the scallop flesh.

5 large purple carrots, 1 orange carrot, 5 scallops (shelled), 1 tsp Dijon mustard, 50 cl water, 50 cl white wine, 25 cl clear spirit vinegar, 250 g white balsamic condiment, salt, olive oil, chervil.

Peel the purple carrots, cut them into 9-cm long chunks and cut them into sheets with a Japanese turning cutter. The sheets should be about 50 cm long. Roll them up and secure them with a piece of string or a rubber band. Combine the water, vinegars and white wine. Pour them into a sous-vide bag and add the carrot rolls. Seal, vacuum, and cook for 25 minutes in a 90 °C/194 °F steam oven. Let cool. Boil the orange carrot until tender and puree it in a blender. Add some salt and the mustard, and spoon into a piping bag. Refrigerate. Cut the scallops in 3 horizontal slices, then in 2 vertically. Untie the purple carrot rolls, trim them, and cut them in two lengthwise. Divide the carrot strips into 3, starting from the core, and cut them into different lengths. To serve, draw a line of carrot puree onto the plates, and cover with a few pieces of scallop. Cover with the larger carrot strips, then add the shorter ones to create a harmonious composition. Season with salt, add a thin stream of olive oil, and decorate with a sprig of chervil.

23 / P. 54

Chervil, fish milt, herring

Two austere products having a gustatory conversation.

25 large bulbous chervil roots, 30 g smoked herring milt, 150 g smoke herring roe, 100 g egg whites, 1 dash sparkling water, 1 dash clear spirit vinegar, 5 egg yolks, 200 g peanut oil, 10 cloves, 500 g milk, 3 lemons.

One day in advance, store the egg yolks in a deep-freezer. Gently heat the peanut oil with the cloves, and leave to infuse. Soak the smoked herring roe in the milk for a few hours to remove excess salt. Brush 10 of the chervil roots vigorously to remove some of the skin, then wash. Using a mandolin cutter, cut the roots into ½ mm slices. Count 6 slices per serving, and marinate them for 12 hours in the juice of 2 lemons. The next day, brush 7 chervil bulbs as above, and wash. Cut 2 of them with a mandolin in 1-mm slices. Select the wider slices from the middle of the roots and marinate them in the clove-scented oil. Still using a mandolin, slice 5 other chervil bulbs as finely as possible, dip them in slightly beaten egg whites, and leave to dry in a dehydrator. Peel the 8 remaining bulbs and cook them sous vide. Blend them into a puree, thinning it with the clear spirit vinegar and sparkling water. Spoon into a piping bag. Drain the smoked herring roe, rinse and dry in a 150 °C/300 °F dehydrator. When thoroughly dry, blend into a powder. Defrost the egg yolks and whisk them with 1 teaspoonful of smoked herring milt, thinning the preparation with a dash of clove-scented oil. Pour into a piping bag. Peel the remaining lemon, cut out the segments, and cut them in to cubes. Shape 2 slices of lemon-marinated chervil into a cone. Pipe some egg yolk mixture into these cones, then fill them with the chervil puree.

Count 3 cones per serving, adding a cube of lemon pulp to the first cone, two cubes in the second cone, and leaving the third cone plain. To serve, place the cones, point side up, on the plates. On top of them, position a slice of clove-scented chervil bulb and the chervil crisps above. Finish with the powdered herring roe.

24 / P. 179

Cherry, green almond

To sublimate its fruity taste, the juiciness of a cherry is enhanced by a gel of sage and a few green almonds.

1,5 kg cherries, 2 kg green almonds, 1 bunch pineapple sage, 1,7 litre spring water, 425 g granulated sugar, 27 sheets gelatin (2 g each, or 200 Bloom), 5 cl white balsamic condiment, 25 g orgeat syrup, 2,25 g ice cream stabilizer, 30 g glucose, 15 g inverted sugar, 200 g dried and peeled almonds.

Tail and pit half of the cherries. Blend them to a pulp and weigh 500 g of it. Make a syrup by boiling 50 g sugar, 20 cl water, the glucose, inverted sugar, and stabilizer. Let cool, then blend with the 500 g of cherry pulp and 2,5 cl white balsamic condiment.
Pour into a Pacojet bowl, and freeze until hard. Run through the Pacojet machine 1 hour before serving. Break the green almonds open, trying not to break the almonds inside. Blend them with the dried almonds into a smooth almond puree. Spoon into a piping bag. Stone the remaining cherries, keeping the stalk on and leaving the fruit as intact as possible. Count 3 cherries per serving. Insert half a green almond into each cherry. Bring 1,5 litre of water to a boil with remaining sugar, and throw the pineapple sage leaves into this syrup. Take off the heat, cover the saucepan with cling film, and let sit for 15 minutes. Soak the gelatin in cold water for 10 minutes. Strain the sage syrup, add the drained gelatin, and let the syrup cool to a lukewarm temperature without letting it set into a jelly. Put the cherries, three by three, into rectangular stainless steel cutters (6 cm x 3 cm x 3 cm) closed at the bottom with cling film.
Pour the jelly to just cover the cherries, making sure the stalks are sticking out above the edge of the moulds. Refrigerate until set. To serve, cut the jelly in order to separate the cherries, cutting in different directions so that the sides have various angles. Arrange them randomly on the plates. On each jellied cherry, add a few drops of white balsamic condiment and orgeat syrup. Put a small knob of almond cream between the cherries in order to place a scoop of sorbet on them. Finally, add the remaining peeled green almonds.

25 / P. 128
-

Beefsteak mushroom

A rare find for a mycologist, brought where nobody expects a mushroom. A dessert. Magical.

1 beefsteak mushroom (Fistulina hepatica), 100 g cocoa paste (100%), 25 cl milk, 250 g cream, 1 vanilla pod, 100 g egg yolks, 200 g sugar, 1 g Super Neutrose (ice cream stabilizer), 10 cl water.

Make a vanilla ice cream : heat the cream and milk the slit and scraped vanilla pod. Whisk the egg yolks and 100 g sugar with the Super Neutrose. When the milk and cream reach a boil, gradually whisk them into the yolks and cook until thickened. Take off the heat, let cool, refrigerate overnight, and pour into a Pacojet bowl. Bring the remaining sugar and water to a boil. To serve, run the vanilla ice cream through a Pacojet machine. Finely slice the mushroom and brush the slices with syrup. On each plate, put a scoop of vanilla ice cream. Cover with mushroom slices, and grate some cocoa paste over the entire preparation.

26 / P. 222
-

mackerel cushion

As if you could take a good bite of the air at the port of Boulogne-sur-Mer.

125 g Manitoba flour, 5,8 cl lager beer, 2 g fine salt, 2 g olive oil, oil for deep-frying, 250 g mackerel, 10 cl milk, 1 large agata potato, 150 g cream (35 % butterfat), 2 g agar-agar, 1 bunch geranium flowers.

In a stand mixer fitted with the dough hook, knead the flour, lager, olive oil and fine salt at speed 2 for 7 minutes. Insert the dough into a sous-vide bag and leave it at room temperature, outdoors, for 3 hours.
Cook the potato in boiling salted water. Peel it, weigh 100 g of potato pulp, and combine them in a saucepan with the skinned and diced smoked haddock, milk, cream and agar-agar. Bring to a boil, and blend in a Thermomix for 1 minute. Rub through a sieve and pour into a siphon. Add two gas cartridges, and keep warm in a water bath. Roll out the dough 1-mm thick. Fold it in two and run it through a dough rolling machine. Cut out 3,5 cm disks with a round cutter and deep-fry them in 210 °C/410 °F oil. Drain the cushions, pierce a small hole into them and fill them with the smoked haddock siphon foam. Stick a geranium sprig in the opening, and serve.

27 / P. 29
-

Cauliflower, bee pollen

A floral crust for a burning hot cabbage flower. And the shock of a chilled pear seasoning.

210 g unbleached flour, 150 g dried bee pollen powder, 20 g fresh yeast, 30 cl milk, 22 g soft brown sugar, 7 g fine salt, 15 g olive oil, 3 baby cauliflowers, 1 normal-sized cauliflower, ascorbic acid, 1 bunch wild chervil (sweet cicely), 2 Comice pears, scallops (shelled), 1 kg unsalted butter, 200 g organic rapeseed oil, fleur de sel, freshly ground pepper.

In a stand mixer, combine the flour, 105 g pollen powder, yeast, 15 cl milk, soft brown sugar, fine salt, and olive oil. Knead at speed 2 for 8 minutes, and keep the resulting dough refrigerated.
Clarify the butter, collecting also the residue and keeping the butter for another use. Cook the baby cauliflowers in boiling salted water, keeping them slightly crunchy at the core. Cool in iced water, drain.
Carve the normal-sized cauliflower with a round cutter, leaving three holes at the top the size of a baby cauliflower. Keep the cauliflower in a damp cloth. Cook the carved-out piece of cauliflower in the remaining 15 cl milk, blend into a puree, season with salt. Roll out the bee pollen dough and wrap each baby cauliflower tightly in it. Bake them immediately at 170 °C/340 °F, seam side down, until golden brown. Meanwhile, dice the pear and keep it in water with ascorbic acid added. Also dice the scallops, and mix both pear and scallops with the residue from butter clarification. Season with fleur de sel, freshly ground pepper and rapeseed oil. Spread the cauliflower puree onto the plates. Throw a few sprigs of sweet cicely onto it. Insert the baby cauliflowers baked in a crust into the holes of the larger cauliflower and bring that at table. Carve each baby cauliflower into 4. On the side, add the seasoned diced pear and scallops, and sprinkle the plate with bee pollen.

28 / P. 97

-

Long choux pastry, grilled broccoli

A long piece of cabbage to share; two diners soaking their bread in the same plate.

25 cl spring water, 4 eggs, 150 g pastry flour, 2 g fine salt, 30 g white chocolate, 1 large head of broccoli, 1 bunch basil, 50 g unblanched almonds, 1 bunch common yarrow, fleur de sel, freshly ground pepper, 2 egg yolks, 100 g clarified butter.

Halve the head of broccoli lengthwise and cook it in boiling salted water. Drain, and sear on one side. Parboil the basil, and blend the seared broccoli and basil together. Season with salt. Make a choux pastry and pipe elongated, éclair-like shapes, 35 to 40 cm long.
Brush the top with egg wash (2 egg yolks beaten with a few drops of water). Grate a little white chocolate over the choux pastry, and bake at 200 °C/400 °F for 14 minutes. Spread the puree onto the plates and stick the yarrow sprigs upright into it. Grate the almonds over this. When the choux are just out of the oven, season them with fleur de sel, freshly ground pepper, and clarifide butter. Serve on a wooden board with a pair of scissors.

29 / P. 32

-

Beeswax, yogurt powder

A frosted beehive. It's raining powder. Bill VIola, again, is not far.

100 g beeswax, 500 g milk, 100 g cream (35 % butterfat), 50 g dextrose, 130 g maltodextrin, 5 g ice cream stabilizer, 20 g powdered milk, 2,8 g fine salt, 95 g granulated sugar, 250 g cocoa butter, 500 g yogurt (0% butterfat), 50 g egg whites, 25 g honey.

Dry the yogurt in a dehydrator, then pulverize in a blender. Make a Swiss meringue by beating the egg whites with 75 sugar and 25 honey in a double boiler until they reach 50° C/122 °F, then off the heat for 10 minutes in a stand beater until stiff and thick. Using a piping bag, shape small meringues on a baking sheet, and dry for half a day in a 60 °C/140 °F oven. Coarsely chop the beeswax with a knife.
Melt the cocoa butter to 50° C/122 °F and add half of the chopped beeswax. Leave in a very low oven or a dehydrator for half a day, keeping the temperature just below 55 °C/131 °F.
Make the ice cream using the remaining half of the beeswax — heat the milk, cream, dextrose, powdered milk, salt, and maltodextrin to 50° C/122 °F. Gradually add 20 sugar mixed with the ice cream stabilizer. Bring to a boil, stir in the chopped beeswax, mix well, cover the surface with cling film, and let sit for half a day. Strain through a sieve, heat to 70 °C / 158 °F, and blend for 2 minutes with a hand mixer. Pour into a Pacojet bowl and freeze until solid. Some time ahead, arrange some ice cubes onto a rack some distance apart from each other. Pour the warm cocoa butter into an automatic funnel and pour it over the ice very slowly in order to obtain some long beeswax drops. When the ice cubes have melted, collect the drops and keep them in a deep-freezer. To serve, make a nice scoop of ice cream and prop it onto the plate with a small meringue. On top, stick a beeswax drop, then sprinkle with yogurt powder.

30 / P. 91

-

Pumpkin, sea bream

Like an aspic of Cucurbitacea.

1 small orange pumpkin (2 kg), 2 sea breams, 50 g agar-agar, 4 saffron threads, 1 bunch common yarrow, 4 g fine salt and 7 g granulated sugar mixed together, 220 g rapeseed oil, 12 g Glice, 25 g milk, 5 egg yolks, 150 g fine salt, 150 g sugar, 0,5 g xanthan gum.

Mix 150 g sugar and the salt. Nestle the egg yolks into this, making sure they're completely covered. Leave them there for 8 hours. Once the egg yolks are conveniently cured in salt and sugar, rinse them, pat them dry, and set aside. Peel the pumpkin and coarsely chop it. Run it through a juicer, collect the juice and the fiber. Dry the fiber in a dehydrator. Fillet the sea breams and cut the fillets into slivers.
Weigh 500 g pumpkin juice, add the agar-agar and the sugar-salt mix. Bring to a boil. Pour this warm jelly into an automatic funnel. Line some very flat, straight-edges baking sheet with cling film and lay the sea bream slivers over them, spacing them 2 cm apart. When the pumpkin jelly's temperature drops down to 45 °C/113 °F, pour it over the fish slivers to barely cover them. Leave to set. Press a round 3,5 cm cutter with your hands into an oval shape, and use it to cut out 6 oval piees of pumpkin jelly. Heat 200 g rapeseed oil and the Glice to 60 °C/140 °F, then refrigerate until set. Warm the milk, add 2 saffron threads, and let sit for 15 minutes. Using a hand mixer, emulsify the gelified oil with the saffron milk. Pour into a squeeze bottle. Weigh 100 g of the remaining pumpkin juice ; add 20 g rapeseed oil, 2 saffron threads, 30 g cured egg yolks, and 0,5 g xanthan gum. Season with salt, and emulsify with a hand blender. This dish should be plated at room temperature : lay 5 jellies into a stack, arranging them in a spiral shape in a staircase fashion. Finally, add the sixth jelly, the pumpkin powder, the saffron-scented rapeseed oil, and some common yarrow sprigs. Serve the sauce on the side.

31 / P. 174

-

Quince

The texture and taste of a fruit you cannot bite in.

6 quince, 2,35 litres spring water, 1,2 kg granulated sugar, 4 g agar-agar, 40 cl unfiltered organic apple juice, 1 Tahiti vanilla pod, 100 g egg whites, 1 tbsp citric acid, 1 lemon, 2 g ice cream stabilizer, 100 g hazelnut oil, 15 g inverted sugar, 0,5 g fine salt.

Peel and quarter the quince, and make a syrup by boiling 2 litres water with 1 kg sugar. Put the quince in the syrup, add a handful of quince peelings and the halved lemon, and cook gently for 1 hour. Let cool in the syrup, then cook for 1 more hour. Let cool — the syrup should take on a red color. Drain the quartered quince, remove the core. Cook 4 quince quarters in a little syrup for at least 30 more minutes, until they become firmer and bright red. Leave one quince quarter in the syrup and puree the three others in a blender until very smooth. Weigh 400 g cooked and drained quince with 100 g of the same syrup, 22,5 cl spring water, the inverted sugar, stabilizer and 2 pieces of lemon peel from the first stage of cooking. Bring to a boil, then refrigerate overnight. Remove the lemon and puree in a blender. Pour this into a Pacojet bowl and deep-freeze. Cut the remaining quince in 5-mm thick slices. Line a raised-edge cooking sheet, about 16 x 22 cm, with cling film, spacing them regularly so that they do not touch each other. Bring the apple juice, 10 cl water, the agar-agar, and the fine salt to a boil. Pour this onto the sliced quince until they're barely covered. Let cool. Cut this jelly into rectangles. Make an Italian meringue — first boil the remaining sugar with 2,5 cl water into a syrup. Beat the egg whites until stiff, add the hot syrup in a thin stream, and keep beating until completely cold. Divide the meringue into quarters. Dry three quarters of it in a low oven and whip the remaining quarter with a little citric acid. Spoon into a piping bag. Pulverize the dried meringue also with some citric acid. Keep in a dry place. Paste the jelly rectangles onto the plate (count 3 or 4 per serving) with a little preserved quince puree, standing them on the narrow side. Pipe a small knob of sour meringue on one side and cover with sour meringue powder. Adjust a quenelle of sorbet on top of the jelly rectangles. Decorate with a few cubes of bright red preserved quince and a streak of hazelnut oil.

32 / P. 205

-

Celery rib and leaf, apple

Pale green on a spatula.

700 g celery sticks, 150 g celery leaves, 2 Granny Smith apples, 1 piece of candied angelica, 75 g egg whites, 125 g powdered glucose, 25 cl spring water, 50 g honey, 20 g butter, 4 sheets gelatin, 240 g cream, 2,2 g xanthan gum, 15 g lemon juice, 10 g icing sugar, ascorbic acid, 200 g sugar.

Run the celery leaves and 200 g celery sticks through a juice extractor. Weigh 200 g of this juice and mix it with 0,7 g xanthan gum and the lemon juice. Make an Italian meringue: soak the gelatin in cold water. Heat 50 g water, the glucose and honey to 120 °C/248 °F. Beat the egg whites until stiff, adding the syrup in a thin stream. When the meringue is quite stiff and still warm, add the drained gelatin and butter. Keep beating until cold. Fold in the celery cream, and spread the meringue evenly in a pastry frame with a 7-mm high rim placed onto a nonstick baking mat. Refrigerate until set. Cut this mousse into 2-cm wide and 7-cm long strips, and lay them over some wooden-handled angled spatulas. Finely dice the remaining celery sticks, one apple, and the candied angelica. Onto the celery mousse, place 4 cubes of angelica. Mix two thirds of the diced celery with one third of the diced apple, and put them into a cold light syrup made by boiling 20 cl water, 200 g sugar, and a pinch of ascorbic acid. Run the last apple through a juicer. Weigh 150 g apple juice, then stir in 1,5 g xanthan gum and the icing sugar. Drain the diced celery and apple, and combine them with the apple gel. Decorate the mousse with the diced apple and celery in gel, and finish the dish by adding a few young celery leaves on top.

32 / P. 205

-

Celery, apple

Al dente squash in a sweet infusion.

700 g celery sticks, 150 g celery leaves, 2 Granny Smith apples, 1 piece of candied angelica, 75 g egg whites, 125 g powdered glucose, 25 cl spring water, 50 g honey, 20 g butter, 4 sheets gelatin, 240 g cream, 2,2 g xanthan gum, 15 g lemon juice, 10 g icing sugar, ascorbic acid, 200 g sugar.

Run the celery leaves and 200 g celery sticks through a juice extractor. Weigh 200 g of this juice and mix it with 0,7 g xanthan gum and the lemon juice. Make an Italian meringue: soak the gelatin in cold water. Heat 50 g water, the glucose and honey to 120 °C/248 °F. Beat the egg whites until stiff, adding the syrup in a thin stream. When the meringue is quite stiff and still warm, add the drained gelatin and butter. Keep beating until cold. Fold in the celery cream, and spread the meringue evenly in a pastry frame with a 7-mm high rim placed onto a nonstick baking mat. Refrigerate until set. Cut this mousse into 2-cm wide and 7-cm long strips, and lay them over some wooden-handled angled spatulas. Finely dice the remaining celery sticks, one apple, and the candied angelica. Onto the celery mousse, place 4 cubes of angelica. Mix two thirds of the diced celery with one third of the diced apple, and put them into a cold light syrup made by boiling 20 cl water, 200 g sugar, and a pinch of ascorbic acid. Run the last apple through a juicer. Weigh 150 g apple juice, then stir in 1,5 g xanthan gum and the icing sugar. Drain the diced celery and apple, and combine them with the apple gel. Decorate the mousse with the diced apple and celery in gel, and finish the dish by adding a few young celery leaves on top.

34 / P. 188

-

Yellow courgette, bee pollen

Sharp-edged and luminous...
The golden yellow of preserved Summer squash and seared whelk.

20 yellow courgettes, 100 g fresh bee pollen, 400 g colza oil, 72 whelks, 10 cl white wine, 100 g white wine vinegar, 100 g preserved citron (domaine Calavas), 70 g rapeseed oil, nasturtium leaves.

Rinse the whelks in plenty of water, then cover them with clear water and refrigerate overnight. Drain and transfer to a large saucepan ; add enough water to cover, the vinegar and the white wine. Bring to a simmer, cook for 15 minutes on low heat, then drain. Take the whelks out or their shell with a wooden skewer. Remove the tough part and the intestines at the end. Finely slice the whelk meat and lay the slices 9 by 9 on a sheet of parchment paper. Fold the paper and keep refrigerated. Peel the courgettes with a potato peeler and put the skins in sous-vide bags with 20 g rapeseed oil. Cut the courgette meat into 5-cm chunks, then into perfect 5-cm cubes. With the tip of a very fine paring knife, cut each cube into 4 L-shaped pieces, 1 cm thick, preserving the original height of 5 cm. At the end of this process, you will be left with a small square piece and four L-shaped pieces of decreasing size. Put all the trimmings in a sous-vide bag, vacuum, and cook for 8 minutes in a 83 °C/181.4 °F steam oven. Let cool, then blend in a Thermomix at speed 10 for 1 minute. Transfer to a fine sieve and leave to drain until thick. Season with salt and spoon into a piping bag. Blend 50 g rapeseed oil and the fresh bee pollen, add the raw courgette cubes and refrigerate overnight. Finely dice the preserved citron. Trim the nasturtium leaves with a 3-cm round cutter. To serve, lay the courgette puree on the plates with a 5-cm square stencil in a 3-mm thick layer. Smooth with a spatula. Place the courgette « corners » onto the puree in a random pattern. Top with 3 cubes of preserved citron, and cover with 3 trimmed nasturtium leaves. Add a few drops of rapeseed oil and, at the last minute, sear the paper with the whelk slices inside for 2 minutes. Season with salt, and skewer the 9 slices together. Serve just as it is.

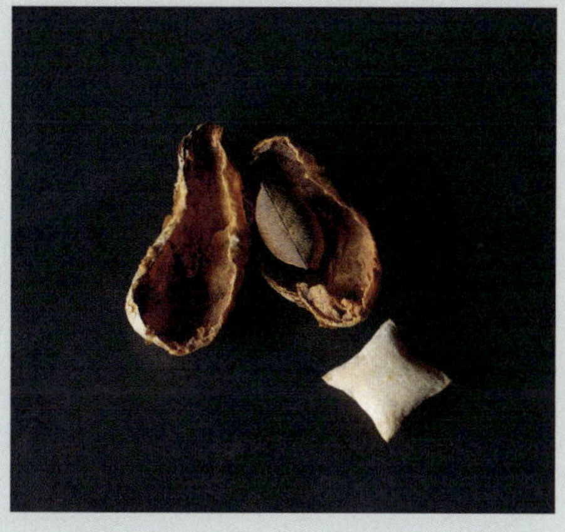

35 / P. 105

-

Potato cushion

A potato peeling turns into flour: an entirely new taste.

2 kg Pompadour potatoes, 900 g pastry flour, 28 g fresh yeast, 50 cl spring water, 20 g fine salt, 15 cl milk, 50 g cream, 15 g organic sunflower oil, 25 g unsalted butter, freshly ground pepper.

Bake the whole potatoes for 1 hour in a 170 °C/340 °F oven. Cut them in two, scoop out the flesh, and run it through a food mill. Bake the potato skins again in the oven at 170 °C/340 °F for 15 minutes, then dry them in a dehydrator. In a saucepan, combine 300 g mashed potatoes, the cream, butter 5 g salt and some freshly ground pepper, and bring to a boil. Add the sunflower oil, and pour into a siphon. Keep the siphon in a hot water bath. Pulverize the potato skins in a blender and weigh 150 g of that powder. Knead it with the flour, water, remaining fine salt, and yeast for 10 minutes at speed 1. Put the dough in a sous-vide bag and refrigerate for 2 hours. Roll it out 2-mm thick, cut out 5-cm squares and throw these onto a burning hot baking sheet in a 220 °C/425 °F oven for 3 minutes. Take them out of the oven, and fill them with potato foam.

36 / P. 234

-

Razor clam, sand fish

Both translucent, the bivalve and the weever.

2 weevers, 600 to 800 g each, 8 large razor clams, 200 g sea lettuce, 2,5 g spirulina, 1 kg peeled potatoes, 20 g salt, 250 g butter, 75 cl water, rapeseed oil.

Make a seawater emulsion : stew 100 g sea lettuce in butter, add some water and strain. Emulsify with a hand blender. Boil the potatoes until tender and mash them with a little water. Run them through a food mill and leave to dry in a 60 °C/140 °F dehydrator for 3 hours. Dry the remaining sea lettuce in a 50° C/122 °F dehydrator, pulverize in a Thermomix for 30 seconds at speed 10. Open the razor clams with a spatula. Collect the muscles, clean the guts and heads. Refrigerate. Gut the weevers and clean the insides. Fillet the weevers and peel off the skin. Trim the ends of the fillets. Cut each fillet into three pieces, then each piece butterfly-like. Open it flat, lay a razor clam muscle along the middle, and fold back. Wrap tightly in cling film and twist the ends. Cook the weever rolls for 6 minutes in a Roner machine set at 48 °C/118 °F. Meanwhile, finely chop the razor clams' heads and guts, cook it for 30 seconds in a 100 °C/212 °F steam oven. To serve, smear some mashed potato onto each plate and add some chopped razor clam heads and guts. Cut the weever rolls in three pieces to expose the cooking. Cover the chopped heads and guts with sea lettuce emusion. Place a spirulina crisp on top of one of the weever chunks, and season with rapeseed oil and a pinch of sea lettuce powder.

37 / P.228

-

Yellow courgette paper

Each shade of colour is a nuance of taste. Revealing the taste in a vegetable skin.

7 yellow courgettes (pick firm, large ones), 100 g preserved citron in its syrup, 2 lemons, 100 g olive oil, fleur de sel, freshly ground pepper.

Slice 4 courgettes into thin sheets using a Japanese turning cutter. Cut these into 7-cm square shapes, and count 3 per serving. Arrange them into stacks, putting the white squares (flesh side) at the bottom and the yellow squares (skin side) on top. Refrigerate. Coarsely chop the remaining courgettes, discarding the seeds. Put them into a sous-vide bag with a dash of olive oil, and cook for about 20 minutes in a 100 °C/212 °F steam oven. Blend into a puree, season with salt, and drain slightly so that the puree is smooth and dry. Spoon into a piping bag. Squeeze the lemons, grate some of the zest into the juice, and use it to make a vinaigrette with the citron syrup, olive oil, fleur de sel and freshly ground pepper.
Sear the courgette stacks on a plancha lined with parchment paper, adding a dash of olive oil and placing a heavy object on the courgette stacks. Let the skin side burn partially.
On the plates, throw a few cubes of preserved citron. Add some olive oil and freshly ground pepper. Cover with a courgette stack, a line of courgette puree, and drizzle with a little vinaigrette.

38 / P. 24
-

Powdered cod

Rillette-like comfort food. The elegance and finesse of dried cod and its salt.

1 back of fresh cod fillet, 1 kg fresh peas (shelled), 100 g crème fraîche, 50 cl spring water, 2 blades fresh sea lettuce, 2 blades fresh nori seaweed, 1 white turnip (leaves on), 1 bunch watercress, 4 g agar-agar, 500 g coarse salt.

Coat the cod fillet in salt for 10 minutes, then rinse, and cook in a steam oven at 55 °C/131 °F for 30 minutes. Cook one third of the peas in boiling salted water. Cool in iced water, drain and puree in a blender. Rub through a sieve. Dry the remaining peas in a dehydrator, pulverize in a blender, then sieve the powder. Steep the seaweeds in hot spring water. Strain the water, season if necessary. Bring it to a boil with the agar-agar and pour into spherical silicone moulds, adding a few strands of sea lettuce. Leave to set, deep-freeze until solid, and unmould. Using a mandolin cutter, cut the turnip lengthwise into 1-mm slices, then cut the slices into 1-cm round disks with an appropriate cutter. Clean the leaves from the turnip and run them through a juice extractor to collect their juice. In a sous-vide bag, combine the juice and the turnip disks. Using your hand, mix 500 g cooked and flaked cod fillet, 200 g pureed peas and the crème fraîche. Shape into balls, inserting a small ball of seaweed jelly inside. Refrigerate until completely set, then roll into pea powder. Place one ball on each plate, cover with turnip disks, watercress shoots, and finish the dish with the remaining pea powder and seaweed jelly balls.

39 / P. 92
-

Fresh farmer's cheese mozzarella, sturgeon roe

A dissonance — sturgeon roe used as a seasoning.

500 g fresh farmer's cheese in its strainer (faisselle), 5 g Algin, 1 litre distilled water, milk, 5 g sturgeon roe, common yarrow.

Mix the distilled water and Algin. Blend in a Thermomix at speed 1° for 1 minutes, then pour into a container. Do not cover the container but run it through a sous-vide machine in order to eliminate any air bubble. Using a spoon, scoop out 9 to 10 g portions of fresh faisselle. Leave them to drain on kitchen paper for 2 minutes, then shape them into balls and dip them into the Algin bath for 30 seconds. Lift them out with a slotted spoon, rinse in clear water and store in milk, refrigerated. On small flat plates, lay a bed of sturgeon roe, put the faisselle ball on top, and top with more sturgeon roe. Decorate with yarrow leaves, and serve.

40 / P. 123
-

Swiss chard green, peach

As if it were cooked in a vine leaf.

6 large Swiss chard leaves with all the green on, 2 fresh cod fillets, 8 flat peaches, 200 g coarse salt, 10 cl white balsamic condiment, 100 g olive oil, fleur de sel, freshly ground pepper, 2 bunches wild geranium (herb-Robert), 200 g grapeseed oil, 30 g butter.

Quarter 4 of the flat peaches and marinate them overnight in a sous-vide bag with the balsamic condiment, olive oil, salt and pepper. Remove all bones from the cod fillets. Entirely cover the fillets with coarse salt. Let sit for 10 minutes, then rinse and pat dry. Cut the chard greens (cut off from the ribs) into 8-cm diamond shapes, counting 2 pieces per serving. Using the trimmings and remaining greens, make a green oil — blend them with grapeseed oil and a bunch of wild geranium. Strain through a fine sieve. Cut the marinated flat peaches into large cubes, setting aside the marinade. Also cut the cod fillets into large cubes. Spread the Swiss chard greens on a clean working surface, veins side down. On each piece of chard green, place 1 cube of cod and 2 cubes of marinated peach. Fold each piece of chard green over the filling. Insert these 'dolmas' into sous-vide bags and cook them in a 45 °C/113 °F water bath for 20 minutes. Finely dice the Swiss chard ribs. Puree the remaining 4 flat peaches and cook the chard ribs in this puree with a knob of butter, keeping it slightly al dente. Take the Swiss chard 'dolmas' out of their bags and serve immediately with a quenelle of peach and chard rib compote, a streak of green oil, and a few geranium leaves.

41 / P. 196

Chicory dandelion, duck fat with the knife

The bare bitterness of a fabric-like leaf, the silkiness of raw duck meat.

250 g high-quality crab meat, 50 cl unpasteurized cow's milk, 20 cl lactoserum, 8,5 g xanthan gum, 3,75 g fine salt, 150 g unsalted farm butter, 125 g egg whites, 38 g rice flour, 1 head of radicchio di Castelfranco, 1,5 g agar-agar, fleur de sel.

Make the milk soba: heat the milk to 80 °C / 175 °F and stir it into the rice flour. Mix well, adding the fine salt and xanthan gum. Blend with a hand mixer. Let cool. When the batter is lukewarm, add the egg whites and blend once more. Roll out the dough between two sheets of parchment paper, and cook on a plancha, or in a 170 °C/340 °F oven, for 5 minutes on each side. Set aside. Bring 150 g lactoserum to a boil with the agar-agar. Leave to set, then blend into a gel. Spoon this into a piping bag and refrigerate. In 100 g foamy butter, gently sauté the crab meat. Season with salt and pepper. Reheat the blinis in an oven or under a grill, spread the crab meat over them, then roll up the blinis into cylinders. Brush them with the remaining 50 g butter, melted and clarified, and count 2 rolls per serving. With the help of a few drops of lactoserum gel, paste some pieces of Castelfranco leaves onto the rolls. Finally, add a little fleur de sel and a few drops of remaining lactoserum.

42 / P. 225

Fig, tarragon

Natural ice cream – the raw fruit frosted, transfigured with an herb.

20 figs from Solliès, 1 bunch tarragon, 20 cl spring water, 40 g granulated sugar, 1,5 g agar-agar, 0,5 g xanthan gum, 100 g cream.

One day ahead, place the ten best-looking figs in a deep-freezer. Scoop out the flesh of the ten remaining figs. Mash it lightly with a fork and mix it with 100 g whipped cream. Refrigerate. Pick out 20 tarragon tops from the bunch and keep them in a damp piece of kitchen paper. Parboil the bunch, cool it in iced water, and pluck out the leaves from the stalks. Bring the water, sugar, agar-agar and xanthan gum to a boil, add the parboiled tarragon and blend with a hand mixer. Strain, and leave to set. Blend once more and spoon into a piping bag. Slice the frozen figs 2-mm thick with a ham slicer. The slices will instantly take on a frosted look; immediately store them in a deep-freezer until serving time. To serve, place a nice quenelle of fig cream on the plate. Cover entirely with the frozen slices. Finally, add a few drops of tarragon gel, plus the reserved tarragon tops.

43 / P. 154

Cocoa, clear spirit vinegar

A thread of grand cru chocolate, sublimated with salt and vinegar. As noble a Caesar.

200 g Carupano 70 % chocolate (Chocolaterie de l'Opéra), 200 g crème fraîche, 4 almond tree leaves, 20 cl clear spirit vinegar (8 % acidity), 2 g Gellan, 15 g sugar, 2,5 cl spring water, 1,5 g fine salt, fleur de sel, 100 g high-quality blanched almods, 30 g orgeat syrup.

Combine 10 cl vinegar, the spring water, sugar and Gellan in a saucepan. Bring to a boil, stirring. Pour into a container and leave to set. Cut into 5-mm cubes. Mix the crème fraîche with the finely shredded almond tree leaves, put into a sous-vide bag, put under vacuum and refrigerate overnight. Rub through a sieve, then whip the cream, orgeat syrup and fine salt to soft peaks. Spoon into a piping bag. Temperate the chocolate, checking the temperature curves, and keep it at 32 °C. Fill a piping bag fitted with a smooth, round n°2 nozzle with chocolate. Fill some dariole moulds, 6,5 cm in diameter, with icy cold water (between 2 °C and 4 °C). Pipe some chocolate spaghetti into that water, wait a few seconds until set, then drain and keep refrigerated. Grate the blanched almonds over the chocolate. To serve, pipe a nice mound of almond cream, put a cube of vinegar gel on top, and adjust the chocolate sculpture onto that. Add a few grains of fleur de sel and a few drops of spirit vinegar.

44 / P. 255

-

Courgette flower, spider crab

Halfway between a vegetable pie and a stuffed flower.

10 large female green courgette blossoms (with tiny courgettes at the end), 500 g shelled spider crab meat, about 20 large whelks, 1 kg fresh pork skins, peanut oil for deep-frying, 2 large green courgettes, fleur de sel, freshly ground pepper, olive oil.

Boil the pork skins in water for an hour, longer if needed. Cool in cold water, drain and scrape as much fat from the inside of the skins.
Lay the rinds flat and dry them in a dehydrator for 24 hours. Take the skins out and leave them at room temperature for 12 hours to let them soak in a little moisture from the air.
Heat the peanut oil to 200 °C/400 °F and deep-fry the pork skins until very crispy. Drain, season with salt while still warm, and pulverize in a blender. Rinse the whelks, parboil them and rinse again. Transfer them to a saucepan of cold water, bring to a boil then simmer for 30 minutes. Let cool in the cooking water, then remove the whelks from their shells. Rinse them and finely dice them. Set aside. Steam the green courgettes until tender, and puree them in a blender with a little olive oil. Drain in a cloth to eliminate excess moisture, then season with salt.
Cut out the courgette flowers from their tiny courgette, and cut these in two slantwise. Discard the pistil from the flowers.
Mix the chopped whelks, spider crab meat and a little green courgette puree.
Stuff the flowers with this. Cook the stuffed flowers and the tiny courgettes for 2 minutes in a 80 °C/175 °F steam oven. Season with salt, brush with olive oil. Spread a little courgette puree onto the plates and add one stuffed flower, propping it with pieces of tiny courgettes on the side. Sprinkle some powdered pig skin in front of the composition.

45 / P. 259

-

Warm strawberry, lemon thyme

An astonishingly warm, tube-shaped ruby.

500 g mara des bois strawberries, 750 g strawberries of any variety, 40 g sugar, 3 g agar-agar, 0,2 g Gellan, 1 bunch silver fennel, 1 bunch lemon thyme, 10 cl spring water, 100 g grapeseed oil, 150 g glucose, 200 g white fondant.

Top and tail the any-variety strawberries, and heat them for 30 minutes in a double boiler until you can collect all their juice.
Dry the strawberry solids in a 50° C/122 °F dehydrator. Measure 20 cl strawberry juice, stir in 2 g agar-agar, the Gellan, and 30 g sugar. Bring to a boil and let cool. Cut the mara des bois strawberries into quarters and divide them between some tube-shaped Exoglass moulds, 2 cm wide and 8 cm long. Cover the underside of the tubes with cling film. Fill them with the jelly at a 50° C/122 °F temperature.
Leave to set, then unmould. Cook the glucose and fondant to 150 °C/300 °F. Pour onto a nonstick baking mat and let cool. Break the resulting sheet, and blend 150 g of it with 150 g dehydrated strawberries into a fine powder. Sprinkle over a nonstick baking mat covered with oval-shaped stencils. Bake at 180 °C/350 °F for 1 or 2 minutes. Unmould the tuiles and store them in a dry place. Pluck out the leaves from half the lemon thyme and add them to the spring water with 10 g sugar and 1 g agar-agar. Bring to a boil, and strain. Let cool, and blend into a gel. Spoon into a piping bag. Pluck out the leaves from half the fennei bunch and blend them with the grapeseed oil. Strain through a fien sieve.
To serve, warm the strawberry aspice in a steam oven for 1 to 2 minutes. On a bed of lemon thyme gel, place one aspic per plate.
Paste a strawberry tuile on the back of the aspic with a little gel, and finish with lemon thyme and fennel leaves. Add a little silver fennel oil.

46 / P. 180

-

Raspberry

The cold has blown a raspberry to a multitude of tiny rubies and scattered them all around.

2 Granny Smith apples, 15 fresh raspberries, raspberry juice, 275 g raspberry pulp, 15 g fresh tarragon, 50 g raspberry vinegar, 5 g xanthan gum, 15 g sugar, 25 g glucose, 2 g agar-agar, 3 g raspberry powder, sweet cicely flowers (wild chervil).

Deep-freeze the raspberries until solid, then break them into small beads. Cut the Granny Smith apples into sheets with a Japanese turning cutter and cut rectangular strips of two different sizes : 14,5 x 5 cm and 8 x 3,5 cm. Marinate them in raspberry juice for 2 hours. Roll into tubes. Make the raspberry coulis : boil 250 g raspberry pulp with the glucose, sugar, and agar-agar. Let cool, and blend until very smooth in a Thermomix. Mix the raspberry vinegar, the remaining 25 g raspberry pulp, the tarragon and the xanthan gum. Leave to set. To serve, fill the apple tubes with raspberry coulis to 2/3 of their height. Top with the vinegar gel, and finish with the raspberry beads, some raspberry powder and a few sweet cicely flowers.

47 / P. 217

-

Wild strawberry, lemon verbena

Fragile and furtive, a light-handed preparation.

750 g wild strawberries, 1 bunch lemon verbena, 50 cl spring water, 75 g granulated sugar, 3,5 g Iota, 50 g cream, 80 g egg yolks, 1 sheet gelatin, 200 g Manitol.

Soak the gelatin in cold water. Make a crème anglaise custard with the cream (instead of milk), the egg yolks and 20 g sugar. When the cream has thickened, add the drained gelatin and some sprigs of lemon verbena. Cover with cling film and leave to set. Rub through a sieve and pour into a piping bag fitted with a round, smooth n°4 nozzle.
Bring to a boil the spring water, the remaining 55 g sugar and the Iota. When the temperature of this preparation goes down to 65 °C / 149 °F, add the remaining verbena leaves (set some aside for final decoration).
Leave to infuse, strain and refrigerate until set. Have the wild strawberries ready.
Cut some regular-sized 5 x 5-cm squares of verbena cream and place them on the plates. Stand the wild strawberries in neat rows onto the cream (five rows of five strawberries each). The cream should be completely concealed by the strawberries. Throw a few lemon verbena tops over the composition. At the last moment, using a stainless steel pick, 'fry' the remaining wild strawberries in the Manitol (melted at about 160 °C/320 °F). Drop them while still hot alongside the dessert. Serve with a spoonful of lemon verbena jelly.

48 / P. 233

-

Summer truffle pancake

Covered in almost-dry soil, or just like.

50 cl raw milk, 20 cl lactoserum, 8,5 g xanthan gum, 3,75 g fine salt, 50 g unsalted farm butter, 125 g egg whites, 38 g rice flour, 60 g Summer truffle, 2,5 g agar-agar, fleur de sel.

Make the milk soba: heat the milk to 80 °C / 175 °F and stir it into the rice flour. Mix well, adding the fine salt and xanthan gum. Blend with a hand mixer. Let cool. When the batter is lukewarm, add the egg whites and blend once more. Roll out balls of this dough between two sheets of parchment paper, and cook on a plancha, or in a 170 °C/340 °F oven, for 5 minutes on each side. Set aside.
Bring 150 g lactoserum to a boil with the agar-agar. Leave to set, then blend into a gel. Grate 25 g Summer truffle over this with a Microplane grater, spoon into a piping bag, and refrigerate. Reheat the pancake, and cover their entire surface with a 4 to 5-mm layer of truffled lactoserum. Fold each one in two, brush with 50 g truffled clarified butter, and grate a generous quantity of Summer truffle onto the pancakes. Season with salt and pepper. Reheat the pancakes in oven or under a gril for a few seconds, and finish the plating with a little fleur de sel and a few drops of lactoserum.

49 / P. 81

-

Spinach cake

A terrine of leaves, an all-vegetable pie.

1 kg large spinach leaves, 120 g pastry flour, 4 eggs, 4 g baking powder, 35 g melted butter, 4 cl milk, 6 g fine salt, 200 g cream (35% butterfat), 1 bunch wild spinach, 1 salt-cured lemon, 100 g snow crab meat, 250 g grape seed oil.

Wash, pick and tail the spinach. Set aside 30 of the larger, best-looking leaves, and keep them refrigerated. Parboil the other leaves in salted water. Cool in iced water, squeeze out excess water, and blend to a smooth puree, then blend in a little grape seed oil. In a large bowl, combine the flour, 2 eggs, 3 g salt, and 100 g pureed spinach. Whisk until smooth, then add the melted butter. Butter some parchment paper, use it to line a terrine dish, then transfer the batter to the dish. Cover the top with cling film, prick it with a skewer in several places, then cook in a 85 °C/185 °F steam oven for 10 minutes. Unmould the flan, let cool on a rack. Mix 200 g spinach puree, 200 g cream, 2 eggs and 3 g fine salt.
Cook this spinach royale in the very same way that you just cooked the spinach flan.
Gently stew the snow crab meat in buter, then stir in 50 g spinach puree. Finely dice the skin of half the salt-cured lemon, and add it to the crab meat. Each cake should be assembled in a springform rectangular pie tin, 4 cm long, 3 cm wide, and 5 cm high. Steam the 30 spinach leaves for 30 seconds. Use them to coat the inside of the tins, vein side inside, making sure they hang over the edge on all sides. Cut the spinach flan and spinach royale to the size of the tins. Lay the flan at the bottom first, then cover with the royale, making sure you don't leave any air bubbles in. Cover this with the crab meat mixture. Lay three layers of spinach leaves over the top, then fold back the spinach leaves to close the cake. Refrigerate for about 12 hours before unmoulding.
Blend the grape seed oil with any remaining

spinach leaves and trimmings, strain and set aside. Reheat the spinach cakes in a steam oven for 2 minutes, then present them to the customer before slicing. To serve, position the slices upright on the plates, sprinkle with green oil, and throw a few sprigs of wild spinach over the plate.

50 / P. 209

-

Gooseberry, radish

Peppery radish, tangy redcurrant – the balance is brought by the marshmallow.

1 litre egg whites, 20 gooseberries, 30 round radishes (pink and purple), 1 head of broccoli, rapeseed oil, salt, pepper.

Make the marshmallow *(see Marshmallow, egg white)*. Cut it into chunks, 1 cm wide and 1 cm long. Finely slice the radishes with a truffle mandolin cutter, and keep between two sheets of wet kitchen paper. Also slice the gooseberries very finely. To serve, align one chunk of marshmallow, 2 slices of radish, and repeat 8 times. On the side, place 5 gooseberry slices ; season with rapeseed oil, a pinch of salt and some freshly ground black pepper. Sprinkle with grated broccoli.

51 / P. 88

-

Gnocchi, lemon, Good-King-Henry

Sweet lemon, standing in the middle of a potato field.

22 bintje potatoes, 22 lemons, 80 g egg yolks, 10 g salt, 50 g grated Parmesan, 150 g flour, 500 g butter, 400 g salt-cured lemon, 300 g Good-King-Henry, 100 g sunflower oil, 100 g rapeseed oil.

Preheat oven to 170 °C/340 °F. Whisk the egg yolks, salt and Parmesan. Set aside. Wash the potatoes, bake them for 1 hour and 20 minutes, then halve them to let the moisture escape and bake them for 30 more minutes. Scoop out the pulp immediately and run it through a potato ricer. Stir 1 kg of the pulp into the egg yolk mix. Sift the flour over this and add the grated zest of 18 lemons. Stir until combined. Divide this dough into 20-g gnocchi and shape them by hand one by one. Store in deep-freezer. Make the salt-cured lemon puree — cover 2 peeled potatoes and the salt-cured lemons with water in a saucepan, bring to a boil, blend into a puree and rub through a sieve. Spoon into a piping bag fitted with a n°2 smooth nozzle. Make a lemon beurre monté : pour 5 cl water in a small sauté pan, and whisk in the diced butter.
The temperature should not rise above 50° C/122 °F. When all the butter is whisked in, add the grated zest of 2 lemons. Mix the oils and grated zest of 2 lemons, leave to infuse, then strain through a sieve. Pour into a squeeze bottle. To serve, cook the frozen gnocchi in boiling salted water, pick them up once they rise to the surface, and toss in the beurre monté. Draw a line of preserved lemon puree onto each plate. On the edge of that line, place one buttered gnocchi. Cover the line with beurre monté and the gnocchi with Good-King-Henry. Sprinkle with lemon-flavoured oil.

52 / P. 84

Large white asparagus, lobster shell

Warm asparagus. The cutting, the plating and the shellfish modify the mousseline sauce.

40 large white asparagus, 280 g clarified butter, 8 egg yolks, 10 blue lobsters (500 g each), 1 head of celery, 1 carrot, 1 onion, 5 lemons, 50 g diced preserved citron (domaine Cavalas), young geranium shoots, 1 fennel bulb, 2 oranges, 1 litre white wine, 50 cl clear spirit vinegar, 5 l water, coarse salt, olive oil, 50 g tomato puree.

Make a lobster stock by bringing the water to a boil with the wine, white vinegar, fennel and a handful of coarse salt. Boil for a few moments, then set aside 40 cl for the bisque. Throw the lobsters into the stock, and boil gently for 5 minutes. Lift the lobsters out of the water, break the claws, throw them back into the stock, and boil for 3 more minutes. Shell the lobsters, break the claws, set aside. For the tomalley powder, boil the lobster tail shells in clear water for 20 minutes until all trace of flesh is gone. Leave in a dehydrator for 1 hour. Pulverize in a Thermomix at speed 10 for 1 minute, then sift the powder through a sieve. Make the lobster bisque : sear the lobster heads in a large saucepan with olive oil for 5 minutes. Add the tomato puree and the diced celery, carrot and onion. Sweat for 5 minutes, and deglaze with 40 cl strained lobster stock. Barely cover with water, add the halved oranges, and simmer for 4 hours. Rub through a sieve, then boil down to one third of the initial volume. Set aside. Finely dice the citron and the lemon pulp (not including any rind). Peel the asparagus and precook them for 5 minutes in a steam oven. Cut them into chunks of different lengths. Make the hollandaise sauce — in a Thermomix, blend 200 g lobster bisque and the egg yolks at 80 °C/175 °F and at speed 3 for 6 minutes. Steam the asparagus for 30 seconds to reheat them, and arrange them on the plates, playing with their different sizes. Top them with 3 cubes of preserved lemon and 3 cubes of lemon pulp. Sprinkle with tomalley powder, and pour some lobster bisque on the plate. Serve immediately.

53 / P. 113

Marshmallow, egg white

Blandness as revealed by a seasoning from the last century.

1 litre egg whites, 1 cucumber, 1 bunch purple cress, 1 bunch forget-me-not flowers, fleur de sel, freshly ground pepper, olive oil, 2 salted anchovies, 2 sea bass roes and milts, spring water.

On a wet working surface, lay a long sheet of cling film. Beat the egg whites until stiff by small quantities. Spoon them into a piping bag and pipe them onto the cling film into sticks, 3 cm wide and 30 cm long. Roll them tightly into the film in order to eliminate any air bubble, and tie the rolls into a knot at each end. Immediately put into a steam oven and cook at 85 °C/185 °F for 8 minutes. Let cool. Take the egg whites out of the cling film and roll them onto the work surface, crushing them gently so as to obtain regular-sized cylinders, 1,5 cm wide. Cut them into different lengths. Take 2 roes and milts from very fresh sea bass. Blend them with the anchovies, a little spring water, olive oil and pepper. The texture should be runny but still somewhat thickish. Refrigerate. Peel the cucumber. Cut it lengthwise into 3-mm slices, then cut out disks, 1,5 cm in diameter, avoiding cutting into the seeds. Count 10 disks per serving. Arrange the egg white marshmallows on the plates. Cover each cylinder with cucumber disks. Season with fleur de sel, freshly ground pepper and olive oil. Complete the plating with purple cress shoots and forget-me-not flowers, and pour the sauce after serving.

54 / P. 66

-

Beans and peas, grey mullet tarama

Seasoned raw products – the juiciness of the beans, the smoky saltiness of the grey mullet.

5 kg snap peas, 200 g egg whites, 100 g grey mullet roe, 1 egg yolk, 50 g fresh bread (without crust), 200 g grape seed oil, 250 g mozzarella di bufala, young shoots of wild arugula from the sand dunes, fleur de sel, olive oil.

Drain the mozzarella and store it in a deep-freezer. Remove the skin from the grey mullet roe. Cook the egg yolk, covered with grape seed oil, at 63 °C.145 °F for 1 hour. In a stand mixer fitted with the flat beater, combine the grey mullet roe, cooked egg yolk, and fresh bread for 3 minutes at low speed, then rub through a sieve to obtain a smooth preparation. If needed, correct the texture with some of the oil in which the egg yolk was cooked. Parboil half of the snap peas, cool them in iced water, and remove the string from the pods. Cut these pods in 1,5 cm chunks, and refrigerate. Cut the remaining raw snap peas in the same manner. Pour the egg whites into a flat container lined with cling film and cook them for 15 minutes in a 83 °C/181.4 °F steam oven. Leave to cool, then blend in a Thermomix at speed 8 for 2 minutes. Season with salt. Add 100 g grey mullet tarama, and spoon into a piping bag. Pick the wild arugula, keeping only the younger shoots. To serve, pipe 8 dots of tarama cream onto each plate. On each one, adjust a piece of snap pea, alternating raw and parboiled pieces and making them stand upright. On 4 of the snap peas, pipe a little tarama in order to paste a few sprigs of wild arugula on top of them. Generously grate the frozen mozzarella over this with a Microplane grater. Season with a few grains of fleur de sel and a little olive oil.

55 / P. 30

-

Herb tempura

A gustatory curiosity – our herbs, wild of garden-grown.

20 cl sparkling water, 1 egg yolk, 160 g all-purpose flour, herbs, oil for deep-frying.

Gently mix the water, egg yolk, and flour. Clean and dry the herbs, dip them in the batter, and deep-fry them.

56 / P. 262

-

Grass herbs 02

The Spring's first grass, freshly cut.

200 g pastry flour, 200 g spinach, 50 g pistachio paste, 8 g olive ol, 4 g fleur de sel, chervil blossoms, red pimpernel, 90 cl water, 150 g inverted sugar, 225 g sugar, 12 g Super Neutrose ice cream stabilizer, 750 g fresh cheese, grass herbs.

Make the grass herb sorbet by boiling the water, inverted sugar, 220 g sugar and Super Neutrose together. Blend and let cool. Stir into the fresh cheese. Place 100 g chopped grass herbs in a Pacojet bowl, add the cheese preparation and run through the machine once. Store in deep-freezer for 30 minutes, then run through the machine again, then repeat the process. Run the cleaned spinach through a juice extractor. Make a green grissini dough — in a stand mixer fitted with the dough hook, mix the flour, 80 g spinach juice, 45 g pistachio paste, the olive oil, and fleur de sel. Knead for 5 minutes, then run through a sous-vide machine in a sous-vide bag in order to enhance the color. Work this dough through a pasta machine at the finest setting, then run again through the spaghetti implement.
Lay the spaghetti flat and straight onto a baking sheet and bake at 160 °C/320 °F for 5 minutes. To serve, run the sorbet through the Pacojet. Add 1 teaspoon water to the remaining pistachio dough, then add the grissini and chervil blossoms. Wrap a scoop of ice cream into this. Place the herb-wrapped ice cream on the plate and complete the plating, making it look as if the sorbet were imprisoned by the green grissini.

57 / P. 56

-

Saffron milk cap, tangerine

An autumnal walk in a forest.

1 kg saffron milk caps, 2 tangerines, 6 apricots, 4 oranges, 100 g red salmon caviar, 350 g butter, salt.

Clean the saffron milk caps very thoroughly so that they do not bleed. Keep the small ones whole and halve the larger ones. Set aside in a damp cloth. Rinse and stone the apricots. Cut them into cubes, and stew them for 15 minutes. Their acidity should be preserved. Arrange them with the apricots in a baking dish. Season with salt. Add 100 g of butter. Make a citrus emulsion : squeeze the oranges, collecting 35 cl juice ; add 250 g butter. Heat to 50 °C and emulsify with a hand blender (fitted with the emulsifying implement). Just before serving, bake the mushrooms in a 170 °C/340 °F oven for 4 minutes. To serve, draw a line of apricot puree on each plate. Add 4 pieces of saffron milk cap and 1 segment of tangerine, then the orange emulsion and a little red salmon caviar.

58 / P. 110

-

Milk, yeast

Massive but fragile. Raw farm product and bakery product brought together.

1,4 litre whole milk, 0,4 kg fermented milk, 70 g egg whites, 240 g sugar, 3 g xanthan gum, 400 g cane syrup, 100 g carnaroli rice, 150 g fresh cheese (40 % butterfat), 200 g preserved blood orante, 500 g fresh cheese (0 % butterfat), 1 cube (25 g) fresh yeast.

Spread the 0% butterfat fresh cheese onto a nonstick baking mat, and dry in a dehydrator at 30 °C. Pulverize in a blender. Rinse the rice in cold water, and cook it for about half an hour in 50 cl milk and 40 g sugar. Let cool, blend to a puree, rub through a sieve. Beat the egg whites to stiff peaks. Fold 75 g 40% butterfat fresh cheese into 150 g pureed rice, then fold in the beaten egg whites. Spread the mixture onto a nonstick baking mat and leave to dry in a dehydrator. Puree the preserved blood orange in a blender with a little of its preserving syrup. Spoon into a piping bag. Boil down 50 cl whole milk with 100 g sugar and the cane syrup, stirring regularly. When this milk jam starts taking on a golden colour, take off the heat, add a little fresh yeast, and pour into a piping bag. Combine the fermented milk, remaining 40 cl milk and xanthan gum. Using a hand mixer, give them a light whizz until foamy. Beat the remaining 200 g egg whites and remaining 100 g sugar to stiff peaks. Fold in one quarter of this meringue to the previous milk preparation, then fold this into the remaining meringue and mix gently. Pour this into a pastry frame with a 4-cm high rim. Deep-freeze. When hard, cut into 4-cm cubes. Return to deep-freezer. Into each bowl, drop a teaspoonful of orange preserve, another teaspoonful of remaining white cheese, and a teaspoonful of yeasted milk jam. Cover with a piece of rice tuile and a cube of milk foam. Sprinkle with some powdered fresh cheese.

59 / P. 192

-

Goat's milk, dandelion

The stable.

1 litre goat's milk, 160 g cream (30% butterfat), 15 g powdered milk, 170 g maltodextrin, 70 g sugar, 150 g dextrose, 10 g ice cream stabilizer, 4,2 g fine salt, 120 g fresh goat cheese, 30 dandelion blossoms; 1 dry, very white goat cheese.

Pull off the pistils from the dandelions and spread the flowers on a sheet of parchment paper. Dry them in a dehydrator into a dandelion 'cotton'. Keep this in a dry place. Combine the milk, cream, maltodextrin, and dextrose in a saucepan and heat to 40 °C / 104 °F. Combine the sugar and stabilizer, add them to the milk. Bring to a boil, take off the heat. Stir in the fresh goat cheese and salt. Blend with a hand mixer and refrigerate overnight. The next day, blend again, pour into Pacojet bowls and deep-freeze. Once frozen, run through the Pacojet machine. On each plate, drop a large quenelle of ice cream. Grate the hard goat cheese over it and decorate with a few pieces of dandelion cotton.

60 / P. 190

Braised lettuce, sorrel

Like the lettuce in a traditional French-style pea dish.

2 lettuces, 2 litres milk, 40 g almond paste, 24 g agar-agar, 400 g fresh sorrel, olive oil, 200 g bread wheat kernels, 100 g toasted buckwheat kernels, 10 cl white balsamic condiment, 10 cl white wine, 5 g salt, extra sorrel for serving.

Simmer the wheat kernels for 20 minutes in salted water, then drain. Bring the vinegar and white wine to a boil, and pour them over the drained wheat kernels. Leave to marinate overnight. Pull off two layers of leaves from the heads of lettuce and keep only the hearts. Wash them in clear water, drain, then quarter them. Keep refrigerated in a damp cloth. Make the almond cream : combine the milk and almond paste in a saucepan. Bring to a boil. Let cool. When quite cold, add the agar-agar and bring to a boil. Leave to set, then divide in two equal parts. Blend one with 200 g sorrel leaves until smooth and light green. Spoon into a piping bag. Blend the other half to the same texture, leaving it plain. Also spoon into a piping bag. Wash the remaining sorrel leaves in clear water, remove the stalk, then tear the leaves with your hands into small pieces (about 3 cm). To serve, sear the chunks of lettuce heart on their three sides on a plancha with olive oil. When they are nicely colored, bake them in a 170 °C/340 °F for 2 minutes. Season with salt. Using a spatula, draw a pattern with the sorrel cream on each plate. Combine the marinated wheat and toasted buckwheat. Place them on one end of the green pattern. Cover the kernels with the braised lettuce, then cover the lettuce with almond cream. Paste the pieces of sorrel leaves onto the almond cream.

61 / P. 101

Langoustine broth and claw

Elusive pearls slipping through your mouth.

Marsh herbs, 1 bunch basil, 1 head of broccoli, 50 langoustines, 1 litre water, 2 tomatoes, 15 g sheet gelatin, 5 g salt, 1 egg yolk, 2 litres peanut oil, oil for deep-frying, 20 cl water, 160 g flour, common yarrow.

40 minutes before starting the preparation, pour the peanut oil into a flat container and leave it in a refrigerator at 3 °C/37.4 °F. Shell the langoustines, set aside the tail shells and claws. In a saucepan, combine the tail shells, quartered tomatoes and water. Boil on low heat for 30 minutes until slightly reduced. Ten minutes before the end of cooking, soak the gelatin in cold water. Strain the stock through a fine sieve – it should be very clear– and immediately add the drained gelatin. Leave to cool until lukewarm. Shell the raw langoustine claws with scissors, up to the second knuckle, leaving the shell on the third knucke. Deep-freeze to facilitate handling. In a deep-fryer, preheat the oil to 170 °C/340 °F. In a bowl, combine the flour, egg yolk and 20 cl cold water. Dip the two first knuckles of the langoustine claw in this tempura batter, and deep-fry for 2 minutes. Drain, paste a few marsh herbs on the claws with a little tempura batter, and deep-fry for 2 more minutes. Finely dice the langoustine tails, and refrigerate. Boil the head of broccoli until tender, then halve it and sear the cut sides on a plancha with a little oil. Puree in a blender until smooth, and spoon into a piping bag fitted with a smooth 2-mm nozzle. Season with salt. Make the langoustine jelly pearls, pouring the jellied stock into an automatic funnel and pour it drop by drop into the cold peanut oil. Leave to set for 15 minutes, drain, rinse in clear water, and refrigerate. To serve, pipe a ring of broccoli puree in bowls. Fill the ring with langoustine jelly pearls. Into the empty spaces, place 3 pieces of langoustine tail and 3 dots of broccoli puree. Cover these with a sprig of common yarrow. Reheat the tempura claws and serve immediately.

62 / P. 249

Nettle liqueur

Our local Chartreuse.

15 nettle branches, leaves on; 1,1 l 40-proof fruit brandy, 150 g sugar, 10 cl water.

In a Mason or Le Parfait jar, collect the nettle leaves after plucking them from the stalks. Immediately pour 50 cl brandy into the jar to preserve the chlorophyll. Leave to macerate for 6 hours. Then, in a saucepan, heat 60 cl brandy, the water and sugar. Pour this into the jar. Leave to macerate for at least 48 hours. The jar should be closed and kept in a dark place, and kept for at least 6 months. A longer keeping time has not been confirmed as yet.

63 / P. 170

Preserved strawberry, hogweed

Like a sculpture of preserved strawberries, and the plant in its own juice.

40 cl spring water, 1 kg gariguette strawberries, 2 kg 'lower-category' strawberries, 325 g sugar, 200 g maltodextrin, anise-flavoured spirit, 2 g NH pectin, 200 g glucose, 3,5 g agar-agar, 300 g white fondant, 1 bunch hogweed flowers, 1 bunch wild chervil.

Hull and halve the lower-category strawberries. Put them in a double boiler with 200 g sugar and cover with cling film. Stew for 20 minutes, then strain and collect the strawberry juice. Keep the strawberries for another use. Cook the glucose and fondant to 150 °C/300 °F. Spread this on a nonstick baking mat and let cool. Once cold, break it into pieces and pulverize it in a blender. Pour the powder into a container. Using a sieve, sprinkle it onto a nonstick baking mat covered with a stencil cut in freestyle shapes. Bake in a 180 °C/350 °F oven for a few seconds, let cool, then unmould the opalines. Pour 500 g strawberry juice into a saucepan. Add 100 g sugar, 200 g maltodextrin, 1 dash of anise spirit and the NH pectin. Cook for 5 minutes and transfer the strawberry gel to another vessel. Make the hogweed blossom and chervil jelly: bring the spring water, remaining 25 g sugar, and agar-agar to a boil. Off the heat, add a few wild chervil leaves and hogweed flowers, cover and let sit. When the temperature of the jelly falls to 55 °C/131 °F, pour it into an automatic funnel and onto the same stencil that you used for the opaline, placed onto a nonstick baking mat. Before it sets, scatter the hogweed flowers and chervil leaves over the jelly it so that they are partly incorporated into it. Hull the gariguette strawberries, cutting a slice at the wider part so that they stand upright. They also should have the same height. Without crushing or damaging them, put them into a sous-vide bag with the remaining strawberry juice. Gently run this through the sous-vide machine and let sit for 1 hour, then drain, and throw the strawberries into the remaining warm strawberry gel. Take them out with a wooden pick — they should be entirely glazed. Place them directly on the plates. To serve, arrange the jelly on the opalines, decorate the opalines with tips of chervil leaves and hogweed blossoms, and adjust one on top of the glazed strawberries. Decorate the sides of the strawberries with a few more chervil tips.

64 / P. 218

Mara and gariguette

Different shades of taste, temperature, and texture.

2 Granny Smith apples, 200 g mara des bois strawberries, 800 g gariguette strawberries, 10 g dextrose, 13 g sugar, 2,1 g agar agar, 1 bunch tagetes (African marigold).

Wash and hull the mara des bois strawberries. Blend them into a pulp and rub through a sieve. Pour into a large, flat container. Peel the apples and cut them into sheets with a Japanese turning cutter. Cut the sheets into 1 x 7 cm strips, dip each one of them in the strawberry pulp, insert them into a sous-vide bag, and vacuum. Roll the strips into 1-cm wide tubes and store in a deep-freezer. Boil the remaining strawberry pulp with the dextrose, 6 g sugar and 1,1 g agar-agar. Let cool, blend with a hand mixer, then rub through a fine sieve. Fill half of the tubes with this preparation. Hull 100 g gariguette strawberries and heat them in a double boiler coverd with cling film, until they have exsuded all their juice. Boil 5 cl of this juice with the remaining sugar and 1 g agar-agar. Leave to set, then blend with a hand mixer. Cut the remaining strawberries into large, regular-sized cubes. Place 3 cubes on each plate, then add 2 filled tubes and 5 empty tubes. Finally, add some tagetes shoots and the strawberry gel.

65 / P. 260

-

Honeydew melon, shrimp

Plain, or pickled. Melon as a seasoned frozen gravel.

3 green honeydew melons, 20 small shrimps, wild black peppercorns, fleur de sel, 1 bunch baby wild cress, 0,5 cl white balsamic condiment, 1 litre spring water, olive oil.

Bring 75 cl spring water to a boil with about 10 crushed wild peppercorns. Take off the heat, cover, let cool, strain, freeze until hard. Break into pieces and crush with an ice crusher. Keep frozen. Peel the melons, remove seeds, and cut the flesh into 1-cm wide cylinders with a tubular cutter. Cut these cylinders into different lengths, counting 8 to 10 pieces per serving. Pick 2 cylinders per serving and put them into a sous-vide bag in the vinegar mixed with 5 cl spring water. Marinate for 30 minutes, then remove from bag. Cut the trimmings into disks of the same diameter as the cylinders (there should be as many disks as cylinders). Shell and devein the shrimps. Cut into 5-mm dice (8 dice per serving). Keep them on cling film stretched over a bed of ice. Arrange the melon cylinders on the plates, including the two vinegared cylinders per serving. On each cylinder, place some diced shrimps and cover with the melon disks. Cover the composition with the baby wild cress and season with fleur de sel and olive oil. Toss the peppered shaved ice with a little olive oil and more freshly ground wild pepper. Serve immediately.

66 / P. 214

-

Smoked mirabelle plum

An aged fruit brandy gives this dessert a patina, and the cream adds a peaty note.

8 mirabelle plums in brandy (see next recipe), 180 g cream, 50 g juniper branches, 50 cl fresh raw milk, 60 g fresh farmer's cheese, 2 g salt, 75 g dextrose, 100 g powdered glucose, 20 g sugar, 2 g ice cream stabilizer.

Burn the juniper with a blow torch until it smokes, then immediately pour 100 g cream through it. Cover with cling film and let sit. Boil 10 cl milk with 80 g cream, the salt, dextrose, powdered glucose, sugar, and stabilizer. Let cool. Blend 10 cm milk with the fresh cheese, and mix both preparations with the remaining milk. Blend with a hand mixer and strain through a fine sieve. Pour into a Pacojet bowl, and deep-freeze. Onto each plate, drop a half-sphere of ice cream, then add some smoked cream and place a brandied mirabelle plum on top.

67 / P. 104

-

Mirabelle plums in brandy

A short-seasoned fruit, preserved in brandy and aged.

1 kg mirabelle plums, 50 cl 45-proof clear spirit, 50 cl mirabelle plum brandy, 2 vanilla pods, 500 g sugar.

Prick the plums with a small wooden pick, and put them in a glass jar. Cover them with the spirit and brandy, add the vanilla and sugar. Close the jar tightly. Place the jar upright in cold water in a double boiler, bring to a boil, remove from double boiler, and let sit for at least 3 months.

68 / P. 141

-

Lemon verbena milk foam

Air, milk, an airy sensation, textureless aromas.

1 litre milk, 3 bushy sprigs of lemon verbena, powdered burnt bread.

Heat the milk to 80 °C/175 °F. Add the verbena, cover, and let sit for 3 minutes. Strain, then heat to 50° C/122 °F. Run through a milk emulsifier, or blend with a Bamix hand mixer until you get a thick foam. Pour onto the burnt bread powder (see Black trumpet mushroom and lichen).

69 / P. 263

-

Frozen mustard, prunes

Icy-sweet mustard, prune like a gentle ointment.

70 cl milk, 300 g cream, 160 g egg yolks, 4 g ice cream stabilizer, 100 g Dijon mustard, 160 g maltodextrin, 3 g fine salt, 160 g sugar, 1 kg stoned prunes, 100 g pistachios, 5 cl spring water.

Heat the milk, cream and maltodextrin to 40 °C/104 °F. Add the stabilizer and 60 g sugar, and bring to a boil. Whisk the egg yolks with remaining sugar until pale and creamy, then add the milk and cook until thickened, stirring. Transfer to a cold vessel to interrupt cooking, add the salt and mustard, blend with a hand mixer and pour into a Pacojet bowl. Refrigerate overnight. Blend again, then freeze. Once frozen, run through a Pacojet machine. Puree the prunes in a blender and rub them through a sieve. Blend 1/4 of this puree with the spring water. Spoon into a piping bag. Spread the remaining 3/4 of the puree to a thickness of 2 mm between two oiled sheets of parchment paper. Freeze. Once frozen, cut out disks of pureed prunes with a 5,5 cm round cutter. Keep frozen. To serve, pipe a little prune puree onto the plate, and adjust a scoop of mustard ice cream onto it. Cover the scoop with a disk of frozen prune and grate the pistachios over the dessert.

70 / P. 98

-

Turnip capsules

A juicy interpretation of the turnip root, Russian-doll style.

100 g white tarama, 4 scallops, 16 turnips, 100 g red cabbage, 70 cl clear spirit vinegar, 50 g sugar, 30 cl water, 20 cl white wine, 2 lemons, 100 g red lumpfish roe, 100 g rapeseed oil, 50 g de Yopol (Texturas), common yarrow, 250 g smoked herring, 1,5 l water, salt, pepper.

Coarsely chop the smoked herring and sauté it in a little olive oil for 1 minute. Add the water, and simmer for 40 minutes on low heat. Strain through a fine sieve and let cool. Make the capsules by hollowing out the turnips with apple corers of different diameters — 10, 15, 20, 25. Transfer the large and medium-sized capsules to the herring stock, and the smaller ones in the vinegar marinade. Smoke the white tarama, spoon it into a piping bag. Finely chop the red cabbage and mix it with the lumpfish roe, remaining vinegar, and rapeseed oil. Cut the scallops into a carpaccio. Into each bowl, put three scallop slices. Pipe some tarama and place the capsules on it (per serving : 1 large one, 2 medium ones, 3 small ones). Add the red cabbage vinaigrette, coat the yarrow leaves in Yopol, and add them for decoration.

71 / P. 77
-

Turnip, cod liver

A fold, a seam.

3 small round turnips, 200 g high-quality cod liver (by J.-C. David in Boulogne sur Mer).

Wash and halve the turnips. Cut their middle part into very thin round slices (less than 1 mm thick). In the middle of each slices, place a small piece of cod liver. Fold each slice in two and secure with a thin skewer. Serve immediately.

72 / P. 87
-

Turnip, langoustine

Harder on the tooth than the crustacean, the vegetable gives it a texture – and the other way round.

2 medium-sized turnips, 5 langoustines, 5 cl walnut oil.

Wash the turnips, peel them if necessary. Cut them into 2-mm thick slices, and put them into a sous-vide bag with the walnut oil. Shell and devein the langoustines. Cut each langoustine tail into three chunks. Lay the marinated turnips onto the plates and add a piece of langoustine on each slice. Curve the slices over the langoustines and thread them together on a metallic skewer, accordion-like.

73 / P. 199
-

Asparagus nests, Stilton cheese

Instant dryness, immediate rehydratation, then the taste bomb explodes.

2 kg white asparagus, 5,5 cl milk, 25 g cream, 55 g Stilton cheese, 1 sheet gelatin.

Peel the asparagus, dry the peelings in a dehydrator, and keep this asparagus 'straw' for serving. Cut the asparagus into julienne strips with a mandolin cutter, and cook them for 1 minute at 100 °C/212 °F in a steam oven. Drain the julienne and, using your hands, shape it into nests, 7-cm wide. Dry them in a dehydrator at a maximum temperature of 60 °C. Store in a dry place. Make the Stilton foam: soak the gelatin in cold water. Heat the milk, cream and cheese without boiling so that the cheese is just melted. Pour into a siphon, add 1 gas cartridge and leave the siphon in a bowl with ice cubes until quite cold. That done, pour a small quantity of Stilton foam into the bottom of an asparagus nest and cover that with another nest. Set this on a bed of asparagus straw, and serve.

74 / P. 71

Smoked lompe eggs, spinach

Where the seasoning plays the main part.

10 large green asparagus from Pertuis (8-12 to a kilo), 150 g black lumpfish roe, 100 g crème fraîche, 1 bunch bear's garlic flowers, 1 bunch bear's garlic leaves, 1 bunch wild chervil (sweet cicely), 1 bunch spinach leaves, 100 g grapeseed oil, fleur de sel, 1 bunch white clover flowers, 50 cl spring water, 1,8 g agar-agar, 1 g Iota.

Trim the asparagus and peel 3 cm at the lower end. Refrigerate. Keep the asparagus peelings and trimmings, but discard the fibrous lower part of the stalks. Cook in boiling salted water, then throw into iced water to cool. Drain and puree in a blender with the spring water. Strain, and collect the juice.
Weigh 200 g asparagus juice, add salt, agar-agar and Iota. Bring to a boil and pour into a small straight-edged baking sheet in a 5-mm thick layer. Leave to set.
Parboil the bear garlic leaves and spinach. Cool in iced water, drain, and blend into a puree with a little grapeseed oil.
Cover the surface of this pesto with cling film and refrigerate. At the last moment, cook the asparagus in boiling salted water for 4 to 5 minutes. Meanwhile, cut one strip of asparagus jelly per serving and steam these for 1 minute. Mix the lumpfish roe with the crème fraîche and a little grapeseed oil.
After taking the asparagus out of the water, brush them with bear's garlic pesto. Season with fleur de sel. Lay the jellies on the plates, and one green asparagus on top of it. Add some lumpfish roe sauce around the asparagus, and throw the chervil, bear's garlic flowers and clover flowers over the dish.

75 / P. 186

Slow-roasted onion on sea salt

The idea of a 'trou normand' in the coal mines of the North country.

8 onions, 1 kg coarse salt, Houlle juniper spirit.

Spread the coarse salt onto a sheet of parchment paper. Place the whole onions, root side down, on the salt. Bake in a 150 °C/300 °F oven for 1 hour. When the onions are very tender, run the flesh through a juicer and delicately strain the onion juice. Serve it chilled with a little Houlle juniper spirit (genièvre de Houlle) during a meal or at the end of it. These slow-roasted onions may be used in many preparations. You should also keep the salt and the onion juices for various seasonings.

76 / P. 206

Raspberry onion

The acidity of a pickle joined to a fresh raspberry.

500 g raspberry puree, 5,5 g agar-agar, 1 litre distilled water, 15 Algin (1,5%), 1 litre spring water, 15 g Calcic, 1 jar pickled small onions in vinegar.

Heat the raspberry puree with the agar-agar, and let cool before blending into a gel. Spoon into a piping bag. Blend the Algin and distilled water, and store in a sous-vide bag to eliminate any small air bubbles.
Blend the Calcic with the spring water.
Cut a slice at the bottom of each pickled onion, and separate their layers, keeping only the larger ones. Stuff them with the raspberry gel, then dip them one by one in the Algin, drain and transfer immediately to the Calcic solution. Rinse in clear water, and store the onions in their pickling vinegar.

77 / P. 236
-

Abalone in a crust

The king of mollusks, just as it is.

8 abalone, 100 g sea lettuce, 5 egg whits, 1 kg fine salt, 400 g unsalted butter, 1 stale round loaf of bread, 4 eggs, 10 heads of barbucine , 6 anchovy fillets, 100 g lactosérum, clarified butter.

Refrigerate the abalone overnight to tenderize them. Rinse well, brush the muscles until clean. Place the abalone in their shells in the steamer basket of a pressure cooker. Put on medium heat, and once the steam valve whistles, cook for 12 minutes. Open the cooker, remove the abalone from their shells while still warm, and discard the innards, but set aside the liver and shell. Brush the outer edge of the shells until clean. On a sheet of parchment paper, put 50 g butter, one abalone and a little sea lettuce. Wrap the paper around the ingredients to make a papillote and insert the papillote into an abalone shell. Mix the salt and egg whites, and cover the papillotes entirely with this paste. Keep refrigerated. Boil the eggs until hard, keep only the whites and chop them finely.
Finely dice the barbucine, add the chopped anchovies and the chopped abalone livers, and mix with a little lactoserum. Season with salt. Using a ham slicer, cut the stale bread into 2-mm slices. Lay them on a sheet of parchment paper set on a baking sheet and cut the bread into 10 cm disks with a round cutter.
Brush with clarified butter, cover with another baking sheet and bake for 6 minutes in a 170 °C/340 °F fan oven. The bread should not brown but remain white. Bake the abalone in their crust at 170 °C/340 °F for 16 minutes. Put a little barbucine salad on the plates and cover with the bread crisp. Open the abalone papillotes, collect the cooking juice and pour it onto the barbucine salad. Finely slice the abalone, and serve.

78 / P. 187
-

Onion skin

All around and at the core, the strength of the onion.

12 sweet Cévennes onions, 5 cl milk, 75 g cream, 2,5 g Metil, 1,5 sheet gelatin, 5 witloof chicory bulbs (endives), 1 g xanthan gum, 500 g coarse salt, fine salt, sugar, 200 g olive oil.

Pour a layer of coarse salt in a baking dish and put 4 onions in their skins on it. Bake at 140 °C/284 °F for 1-1/2 hour. Peel the onions, setting aside some of the skin and covering it with the olive oil. Puree the flesh in a blender. Soak the gelatin in cold water. Weigh 200 g of onion puree, add the cream, xanthan gum and Metil. Blend until smooth. Heat the milk and dissolve the drained gelatin in it. Pour this over the onion puree and blend until smooth. Season with salt, pour into a siphon and add one gas cartridge. Refrigerate. Finely slice 2 onions, brown them in a dry pan. Season with a little coarse salt picked from underneath the onions in the baking dish. Stir on medium heat until dry, and take off the heat when the onions are light brown. Dry in a dehydrator, then pulverize in a blender. Sieve the powder, keep in a dry place. Select 20 nice witloof chicory leaves, keeping only the yellow part. Keep in damp kitchen paper. Braise the remaining endives in a little water, salt and sugar. Peel the 6 remaining onions, halve them and separate their layers. Put these onion 'cups' in a saucepan, cover with cold water, bring to a boil and simmer on very low heat for 20 minutes. Let cool slightly, drain, arrange the onion cups on nonstick baking mats and leave to dry in a dehydrator. To serve, place a 5-cm high and 5-cm wide round cutter on the plate. Into each cutter, drop a piece of braised chicory, fill it with onion crisps and chicory leaves, keeping them vertical. Fill the entire remaining space with onion foam, which will help the composition to stand upright. Season with the onion powder and smoky onion-infused olive oil.

79 / P. 140
-

John Dory skin, anchovy

Sharing some fried fish, but only its skin.

8 John Dory skins (from 4 John Dories), 1 litre cream, 15 anchovy fillets, fresh seasonal herbs.

Fillet the John Dories and peel off their skin (you may use the fish in another recipe). Scrape the skins with a spoon, then dry them in a dehydrator at 65 °C/149 °F for 3 hours. Deep-fry the skins in a 180 °C/350 °F oil until crispy. Drain and set aside. Make the anchovy cream: boil down the cream by half, then add the anchovy fillets. Blend until smooth, and refrigerate until quite cold and thick. Spoon into a piping bag, then pipe the cream onto the plate. Cover with a John Dory skin, and decorate with fresh herbs.

80 / P. 266

Burnt peach

The violence of a blowtorch is needed to harmonize the ingredients.

8 peaches, 4 yellow beets, 10 cl white wine, 100 g white balsamic condiment, 50 g white tarama, 2 lemons, 100 g egg whites, 20 g sugar, 5 g salt, olive oil.

Preheat oven to 200 °C/400 °F. Carefully wrap the lemons in sheets of aluminium foil (they should be completely isolated), and bake them for 12 hours — they should be completely dry. Line a small container with cling film, pour in the egg whites, and cook in a 83 °C/181.4 °F steam oven for 15 minutes. Let cool, then blend in a Thermomix at speed 4 for 1 minute until perfectly smooth. Stir this into the tarama and spoon into a piping bag. Make the marinade : in a saucepan, combine the white wine, white balsamic condiment, salt, sugar, and enough water to cover the beets. Bring to a boil. Clean, peel the beets, slice them 2 mm thick, and leave them in the marinade for 12 hours. Peel and quarter the peaches, remove the stones, and cut each quarter into 3 wedges crosswise. Bake the peaches in a 170 °C/340 °F oven for 3 minutes. Just out of the oven, brush them with olive oil. Burn on each side with a blow torch. To serve, pipe 3 dots of tarama cream. On each dot, place one piece of burnt peach, then dot each piece of peach with a little tarama cream. Cover with beet slices in a harmonious pattern.

81 / P. 139

Potato yarn balls

Strings into crisps, crisps into strings, and fragrant ashes.

1 bintje potato or any floury potato, 1 organic lemon, fleur de sel, oil for deep-frying, coarse salt.

Wrap the lemon in aluminium foil and place it on a bed of coarse salt on a baking sheet. Bake at 200 °C/400 °F for 4 and a half hours, then finish drying the lemon in a dehydrator. Brush the potato vigorously to remove some of the skin, then wash, and shred into vermicelli with a Japanese turning cutter. Do not rinse. Shape these vermicelli into small balls, and insert them into snap-style ball-shaped mesh tea strainers. Quickly deep-fry in 170 °C/340 °F before the potato discolors, unmould, and immediately season with salt. Collect the potato balls on a folded cloth and generously grate some burnt lemon onto them. Serve warm.

82 / P. 106

Smoked herring roe fritters

The title says it all.

250 g all-purpose flour, 8 g fine salt, 30 g sugar, 150 g eggs, 150 g butter, 5 g fresh yeast, 200 g smoked herring roe, oil.

In a stand mixer fitted with the hook implement, combine the flour, salt, sugar, eggs and fresh yeast. Knead for 10 minutes until you get a smooth brioche dough. Add the butter and 50 g smoked herring roe, then knead at speed 2 until the dough no longer sticks to the bowl. Refrigerate the dough for 2 hours, then shape it into small balls and leave to raise for 30 minutes. Deep-fry in oil at 180 °C / 350 °F. Pat the balls dry and roll them in the remaining smoked herring roe. Serve warm.

83 / P. 64
-

Fresh peas, pickled onion

A quick snapshot of Stéphane's greenhouse.

2 kg fresh peas, 300 g plaice fillets, 700 g small pickled onions in vinegar, 1 grapefruit, common yarrow, rapeseed oil, olive oil, 5 g ascorbic acid, 10 g xanthan gum, salt.

Shell the peas and parboil them in a large saucepan of water for 6 minutes. Cool them immediately under cold running water. Run the pea pods through a juicer, and add the ascorbic acid to prevent discolouring. Blend 50 cl of this juice with the xanthan gum, run through a sous-vide machine to eliminate any air bubbles, then pour into a piping bag. Peel the grapefruit, and extract the pulp with your hands. Add a little olive oil and refrigerate. Remove the skin from the plaice fillets, and cut the meat into 1-cm cubes. Halve the onions, and peel them, keeping only the two outer layers. Fill these with the pea pod jelly. Peel 100 g fresh peas, season them with salt and olive oil, and add the grapefruit pulp. To serve, place 4 cubes of plaice on each plate, spacing them well. Add 6 pea-filled onion shells, 3 empty onion shells, and a little fresh pea salad. Finish with a few sprigs of yarrow and a few drops of rapeseed oil.

84 / P. 159
-

Crab, black radish

A crumpled piece of cloth, hardly cooked.

5 brown crabs or spider crabs, 2 large black radish, 350 g unsalted butter, 55 cl spring water, 2 g Sucro, 1,4 g Iota, fine salt, 2 shallots, 1 fennel bulb, clear spirit vinegar.

Cook the crabs in boiling salted water with a little clear spirit vinegar and the quartered fennel bulb. Drain, let cool, shell the crabs. Set aside the crab meat. Boil some of the inside shells with 20 cl spring water, cover and leave to infuse for a few minuts. Strain, add the Iota, and let cool. Rub the black radish with a hard brush to remove some of their skin (they should have a marbled black-and-white look), then cut them into thin sheets with a Japanese turning slicer. Cut out some 8-cm squares in the radish sheets, put them into a sous-vide bag with 50 g diced butter. Cook in a steam oven for a few minutes, then keep the bag in ice. Make the beurre noisette emulsion: cook 250 g butter until light brown, and immediately cool it down by adding the remaining 35 cl spring water. Add the fine salt and the Sucro. Blend with a hand mixer. Finely slice the shallots, sauté them in the remaining 50 g butter. Add the crab meat and take off the heat. Gently stir in the crab shell infusion gel. On the plate, drop a spoonful of this mix, cover with two squares of black radish, steamed until warm. Make three layers of that preparation. Finish the plating with a little beurre noisette foam.

85 / P. 144
-

Oyster mushroom, scallion

Defoliating the woods.

15 large eryngii mushrooms, 200 g cashew butter, 30 cl spring water, 100 g scallion greens, 1 ball fresh lichen, 1 ball fresh green wood moss, 2,5 g agar-agar, 0,5 g xanthan gum, 3,5 g fine salt, olive oil, fleur de sel.

Using a ham slicer, cut the mushrooms into 1,5 mm slices. Count about 15 slices per serving. Finely dice the remaining mushrooms and the trimmings into a duxelles. Stew the duxelles for 10 minutes with a little water in a saucepan, then stir in the cashew butter. Mix well, and spoon into a piping bag. Parboil the scallion greens, and drain. Thoroughly clean the wood moss from any sand or soil. Bring the spring water to a boil, add the moss, cover with cling film and let sit until infused. Add the scallion greens and blend with a hand mixer. Strain through a fine sieve. Add the agar-agar and salt, and bring to a boil. Leave to set, add the xanthan gum, then blend with a hand mixer until you get a clear green gel. Lay the mushroom slices on a baking sheet, cover with a rack, and leave for 1 to 2 minutes in a steam oven. Take them out of the oven. On each slice, place a small mound of cashew duxelles, and roll it up. On each plate, spread the scallion gel. Gently reheat the mushroom rolls under a grill, and place them upright on the gel. Fill the top of the rolls with the same gel, and stick some fresh lichen sprigs into it. Season with fleur de sel and olive oil.

86 / P. 134

Almond feather

Rye like a raw bread dough, enlivened by toasted almonds.

40 g green almonds (unpeeled), 20 g green almonds (peeled), 86 g rye flour, 81 cl water, 5 g icing sugar, 8 g sunflower oil, corn oil, 310 g butter, 1 cl milk, 1/4 vanilla pod, salt and pepper, 100 g hazelnuts.

Cut the unpeeled green almonds into thin slivers and set aside the skins. Cut each peeled green almond in four. Make the feathers : mix 50 g rye flour, 5 g icing sugar, 10 g butter and 6 cl water, and roll out thinly on a sheet of parchment paper. Scatter the slivered green almonds over this. Transfer to a plancha using the parchment paper and brown the dough side through the paper. Then turn the dough over and brown the almond side. Brush with corn oil, season with salt. Blend 50 g softened butter with the milk and 1/4 vanilla pod. Put the remaining butter in a saucepan with the almond peelings and the quartered almonds. Heat gently. Make another rye dough by mixing 36 g rye flour, 10 cl water and the sunflower oil. Pour into a piping bag fitted with a n°3 smooth nozzle, and use this to draw a line onto each plate. Make a hazelnut butter emulsion — mix 250 g butter, the hazelnuts and 75 cl water. Keep at a temperature of 50° C/122 °F and emulsify with a hand blender. In the middle of the plate, drop the butter-vanilla-almond mixture. Cover with the hazelnut butter emulsion, and finish with the almond feather.

87 / P. 151

Snap pea, nasturtium

Egg, chlorophyll, and pepper as a green leaf.

10 quail's eggs, 100 g snap peas, 500 g fresh peas, 100 g very fine green beans, 50 g fresh young broad beans, 600 g cream (35 % butterfat), 1 bunch nasturtium leaves, 250 g sunflower oil, 1 dash hazelnut oil, fleur de sel, 1 bunch flatleaf parsley, 5 cl clear spirit vinegar.

Shell the peas, set aside the pods. Keep a few peas for the finishing touch (1 tsp per serving) and cook the remaining peas in boiling salted water. Puree in a blender with a little hazelnut oil. Season with salt, and spoon into a piping bag fitted with a round, smooth n° 3 nozzle. Put the pea pods through a juicer and keep the juice in a squeeze bottle. Parboil the parsley. Cool it in iced water, then puree in a PacoJet. Heat the sunflower oil to 180 °C/350 °F and gradually pour it onto the parsley puree while blending with a hand mixer. Collect the green oil through a sieve. Cook the quail's eggs in boiling salted water with a little vinegar added for 1 minute and 20 seconds. Let cool, shell. Cook the peas, broad beans and green beans for 15 to 30 seconds in boiling salted water, keeping them green and crispy. Cool in iced water. Dice the green beans. Pull out the string from the snap peas, cut these into chunks. Boil down the cream by half, and add a little green pea pod juice until it takes on a deep green color. Quickly reheat the peas, green beans, broad beans, and quail's eggs, and toss them in the green cream. Season with salt. At the last moment, add the snap peas. Draw a freestyle shape on each plate using the piping bag, making sure the ends meet. Inside the contour, place the quail's eggs and peas. Gently pour the sauce within the contour, without overflowing, and decorate the edges with green parsley oil. Decorate with upside-down nasturtium leaves.

88 / P. 261

Bee pollen, citron

After receiving some stuff from our friend Mauro.

40 g popcorn maize kernels, 50 g maltodextrin, 115 g sugar, 3 g ice cream stabilizer, 45 g honey, 150 g fresh cheese, 6,5 cl water, 12,5 cl milk, 38 g butter, 1 g Super Neutrose (ice cream stabilizer), 120 g fresh bee pollen, 50 g soft dried apricots, 1 citron, 10 g cream.

Make a bee pollen ice cream. In a saucepan, heat the milk, cream, and 25 g maltodextrin. Mix 25 g sugar with the stabilizer, and sprinkle this into the warm milk, whisking well. Bring to a boil, take off the heat, add 40 g fresh bee pollen and the fresh cheese. Blend with a hand mixer, pour into a Pacojet bowl, and freeze until hard. Put the maize kernels in a dry pan on medium heat, cover, and wait until all the kernels are popped. Pulverize them into a Thermomix until you get a regular, fine meal. Make some bee pollen muesli: cook 40 g sugar with 1,5 cl water, the butter and the milk to 115 °C/239 °F. In a stand mixer fitted with the flat beater, combine the popcorn meal, 50 g fresh bee pollen and the diced dried apricots. Add the honey and beat for a few seconds until mixed. Roll out the muesli 2-mm thick between two sheets of parchment paper, and store in a deep freezer. To make the bee pollen caramel, cook all the following ingredients to 106 °C/223 °F: the remaining 50 g sugar, 5 cl water, 25 g maltodextrin, 15 g fresh bee pollen, and Super Neutrose. Pour into a squeeze bottle. Run the bee pollen ice cream through a Pacojet machine, then pour it directly onto the bee pollen muesli in a regular 5-mm layer. Return to the deep-freezer until hardened. Cut it into 1-cm wide strips and cut these to different lengths. Return to deep-freezer. To serve, pipe a large drop of bee pollen caramel onto each plate, and place the iced muesli strips upright onto the caramel, joining their edges together so that they stand like little towers of different heights. Generously grate some citron rind over that, and scatter with a few remaining grains of fresh bee pollen.

89 / P. 175

-

Clochard apple, quince

A nest of jam and compote, carefully hidden from view.

15 reinette clochard apples, 2 Jonagold apples, 160 g apple juice, 80 g sugar, 200 g cream, 4 g Super Neutrose ice cream stabilizer, 2,5 g salt, 310 g de quince syrup, 17,2 cl spring water, 15 g glucose, 3 g xanthan gum, 1 kg distilled water, 5 g Algin, preserved quince puree.

Peel the Jonagold apples and cut each one into six wedges. Cook 80 g sugar into a caramel, add the apples and cook for 20 minutes on low heat. Let cool, then weigh 230 g of this caramelized apple sauce, add 6 cl apple juice and 200 g cream. Blend with a hand mixer. Boil the remaining apple juice with the Super Neutrose and salt. Add this to the previous mixture. Pour into Pacojet bowls, freeze until solid, then run through a Pacojet machine. With hand mixer, blend the syrup, water, glucose, and xanthan gum for 3 minutes. Vacuum to eliminate any air bubbles, then blend the distilled water and Algin. Using a teaspoon, drop the quince syrup mixture into the Algin bath. Leave to set, then lift out the pearls with a slotted spoon, rinse, and set aside. Cut 5 clochard apples into large sheets using a Japanese turning cutter. Make sure you make one single sheet from each apple. Roll these around 1-cm wide plastic tubes, counting one sheet for two servings (the length of the tube + apple should not be above 4,5 cm). Hollow out the ten remaining clochard apples : first insert a round cutter vertically at the flower end 3/4 of the way, then hollow out the apples with an apple corer. Leave the stalk on. To serve, place one apple cylinder on the top part of the plate. Smear some quince puree in the middle of the cylinder, cover with a scoop of Tatin ice cream, and finally add a quince pearl on top. Hide this under the hollowed-out apple.

90 / P. 265

-

Potato, praliné

Like the flaky heart of a leek; nuts as arte povera.

6 large potatoes (agata or bintje), 2 litres peanut oil for deep-frying, 250 g large-leaf mustard greens, 250 g blanched almonds, 250 g hazelnuts, 50 g salted peanuts, 150 g clarified butter, fleur de sel, fine salt, black pepper, 2 bunches young arugula shoots.

Make the salted praliné some time ahead. Combine the almonds, hazelnuts and peanuts on a sheet and toast them lightly in a 170 °C/340 °F oven. Let cool. Blend all the dried fruits together once, then refrigerate them for 1 to 2 hours before blending again until smoother and more fluid. Season with fine salt and freshly ground black pepper, and store in a tightly closed container. Parboil the mustard leaves for a few seconds and cool them in iced water. Drain, and puree in a blender with a little peanut oil. Pour into a piping bag and set aside. Peel the potatoes and cut them into thin sheets with a Japanese turning cutter, throwing the sheets in cold water as you work in order to avoid oxidation and eliminate excess starch. Drain the potato sheets and roll them up tightly into 3-cm wide cigar shapes. Tie each roll with string to keep it quite tight. Count one roll per serving. Keep the rolls in clear water. Start the cooking shortly before serving. Preheat the peanut oil to 175 °C/347 °F in a deep-fryer; while it heats, cook the potato rolls in a 100 °C/212 °F steam oven for 8 to 10 minutes. Test their doneness with a larding needle; they should be tender to the core. Once out of the oven, cut them in two lengthwise and deep-fry them while still hot (to avoid discolouring). When nice and brown, pat them dry with kitchen paper, remove their first layer and cut each half-roll in two — one larger piece and one smaller piece. To serve, rehat the potato rolls in the oven, brushing them generously with clarified butter, and season with salt and pepper. On the plates, pipe a few drops of green mustard puree. Adjust the potatoes onto them with the flaky part to the front. Decorate with the arugula shoots, and, just before serving, add a spoonful of salted praliné on one side of the composition.

91 / P. 208

-

Apple, langoustine

Saturate a fruit with its seasoning.

4 Jazz or Jonagold apples, 40 langoustines, 2 litres peanut oil, 250 g olive oil, about 15 lobster heads, 1 bunch common yarrow, agar-agar, fleur de sel.

Sear half of the lobster heads in a little olive oil until red, then break them with a rolling pin, cover them barely with water and simmer for 3 hours on low heat. Strain through a fine sieve and boil down by half. Measure the reduced stock and add 40 g agar-agar for every litre. Bring to a boil, pour into a container and leave to set. Once cold, grate coarsely with a Microplane grater directly onto a nonstick baking mat and leave at 60 °C/140 °F in a dehydrator until quite dry. Store the dried lobster flakes in a tightly closed container. Sear the remaining lobster heads in a low-rimmed saucepan, break them with a rolling pin and cover with peanut oil. Leave for 1 hour on low heat. Strain the oil through a sieve, then through muslin. Shell and devein the langoustines. Cover the tails with cling film and refrigerate. Put the shells and heads into a saucepan, cover barely with water, bring to a boil and simmer on very low heat for about 30 minutes. Strain through a fine sieve, then boil down slightly until bright orange and translucent. Measure the stock, and add 5 g agar-agar for every litre. Wash the apples, cut a slice at the bottom so that they stand upright. Using a cylindrical, 4-cm wide cuter, cut the apples into half-moon-shaped slivers, keeping the skin on. In a plastic container, soak the apple slivers in a mix of shellfish oil (2/4), peanut oil (1/4) and olive oil (1/4), making sure they are completely covered in oil. Put the entire container in a sous-vide machine and run the machine in order to mix the flavours. Marinate the apples in the oil for 1 more hour, then drain. Arrange them upright on the plates, propping them on each other, and nestle the langoustine tails in the apples. Add a few spoonfuls of langoustine jelly, a few sprigs of yarrow, some fleur de sel, lobster flakes, and a few drops of shellfish oil.

92 / P. 247

-

Green apple, langoustine

Painstaking plating, precise pairing.

3 Granny Smith apples, 16 langoustines, 2 bunches flatleaf parsley, 20 cl peanut oil, 50 smoked pike roe, 25 cl apple juice, 2,6 g agar-agar, corn oil, sat, ascorbic acid, burnet leaves.

Parboil a bunch of parsley, drain and squeeze dry in a clean tea towel. Blend in a Thermomix. Heat the peanut oil to 170 °C/340 °F and to the parsley, with the motor still running. Keep blending for 10 minutes. Rub through a fine sieve, squeeze in a towel to collect the green oil, and pour into a squeeze bottle. Peel the apples and cut two of them into thin sheets with a Japanese turning cutter. Cut out eight 3 cm x 10 cm strips and eight 5 cm x 12 cm strips. Keep in a water bath with a little ascorbic acid. Drain, pat dry, and cover with green oil. Roll up the small strips into cylinders and insert them into 1-cm wide tubes. Roll up the larger strips and insert them into 2-cm wide tubes. Smoke these tubes for 1-1/2 minute. Make a langoustine tartare : shell the langoustines and cut them into 5-mm cubes. Mix these with the pike roe, add a drop of corn oil, and season with salt. Cut the remaining apple into a sheet with the same turning cutter, sprinkle it with the green oil. Roll into a 2-cm wide cylinder and cut it into 8 slices to top the larger apple cylinder. Blend the apple juice with the second bunch of parsley. Pour into a saucepan, add the agar-agar, bring to a boil, strain, and keep in a squeeze bottle. On each plate, position two cylinders of different lengths upright, top the higher cylinder with the smaller apple slice. Add the the langoustine tartare, the apple gel, a little green oil, and burnet leaves.

93 / P. 230

-

Red kuri squash, smoked haddock

Monochromy.

3 medium-sized red kuri squash, 1 fillet of smoked haddock (skinned and diced), 250 g argan oil, 50 g cream, 250 g unsalted butter, 3 kg oranges (to juice), 150 g all-purpose flour, 25 g Parmesan cheese, 40 g egg yolks, 5 g fine salt.

Bake 2 of the kuri squash, wrapped in aluminium foil, for 1 hour in a 170 °C/340 °F oven. Take them out of the foil, quarter them, remove the seeds, and bake for 15 to 20 more minutes at 150 °C/300 °F to dry the pulp a little. Scoop out the pulp and rub it through a sieve. Weigh 500 g of it and mix it with the egg yolks, fine salt, and Parmesan.
Add the flour, stir until combined, and keep half of this dough in a piping bag.
Shape the remaining dough into hazelnut-sized balls. Skin the haddock, separate the yellow part from the white part of the flesh, and dice the white part. Place a dice of smoked haddock into each small ball of dough. Cut the yellow part into small, very thin slivers and set them aside for serving. Once the gnocchi are made, freeze them. Juice the oranges, boil down the juice to a third of its initial volume.
Dice the butter and whisk it with a little warm water on low heat until you get a beurre monté.
There should remain about 200 g squash pulp — using a hand mixer, blend it with the cream until smooth. Spoon into a piping bag fitted with a smooth round N°3 nozzle.
On a ham slicer, cut the remaining raw kuri squash into thin slivers, and keep these in very damp kitchen paper. Pipe the gnocchi dough from the bag through your fingers, giving it irregular shapes, and throw these shapes into boiling water. Once cooked, drain, and pour some argan oil over them.
Then, in the same boiling water, cook the frozen gnocchi. When they rise to the surface, remove them with a slotted spoon, drain. Add the reduced orange juice to the beurre monté, and toss all the gnocchi (regular-shaped and misshapen) in the butter, coating them well. To serve, draw a freestyle shape on each plate with the creamed squash puree, making sure that the ends meet. Position the gnocchi inside that contour, and pour the orange butter so that the entire shape is filled. Sprinkle generously with argan oil, then cover the gnocchi with haddock slivers and squash slivers.

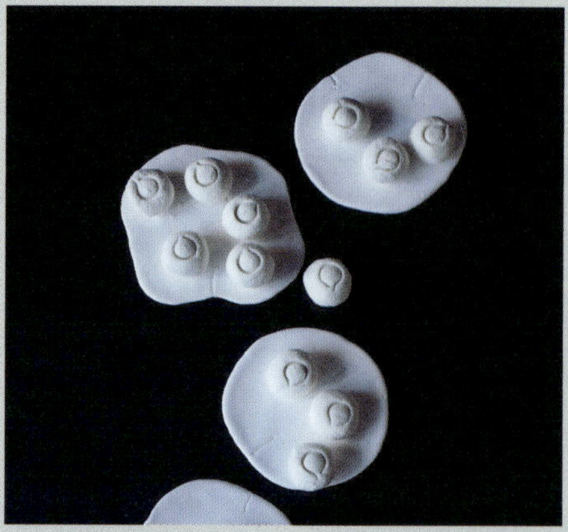

94 / P. 132

-

Roast chicken

A child's memory, an amazement...
Just the roast chicken of Sunday lunch.

300 g raw chicken skins, 25 g butter, 50 g peanut oil, 25 g Malto (Texturas), 1,8 g fine salt.

Spread the chicken skins quite flat on a baking sheet with the peanut oil and butter.
Bake for 30 minutes in a 170 °C/340 °F oven.
Just out of the oven, gather all the chicken fat ans skins in a saucepan, cover and cook for 30 minutes. Take off the heat and let cool.
When the chicken fat is cold, weigh 55 g of it and mix it with the Malto and fine salt.
Knead with gloved hands. Cut some of the crispy chicken skin into small squares.
Shape the chicken fat dough into 2 g balls.
Insert a square of chicken skin into each small ball. Roll each ball between your palms until it is perfectly regula. Make a mark on the top with a small hook. Eat at room temperature.

95 / P. 153
-

First peas

The horn of plenty of early Spring.

100 g flour, 27 cl milk, 12 g salt, 10 g Trisol, 1 egg, 1 bunch parsley, spring water, 100 g cream, 3 g Metil, 1 grapefruit, 1 kg fresh peas (shelled), 100 g cod's liver, a few sprigs of vetch (Vicia sativa), 20 g preserved citron (domaine Calavas), rapeseed oil.

Cook 900 g peas in plenty of boiling salted water. Drain, blend, and rub through a fine sieve. Parboil and peel the remaining peas. Set aside. Blend the parsley leaves into a green paste with a little water. Make the crêpe batter by mixing 100 g flour, 22 cl milk, 5 g salt, 10 g Trisol, 1 egg and 50 g green paste. Leave to rest. Mix 500 g pureed peas with 5 cl milk, 7 g salt, and 3 g Metil.
Add the cream. Pour into a siphon, add 2 gas cartridges. Heat an oiled takoyaki pan and pour the batter into it. Sear it for seconds, pour out excess batter, cook for 10 more seconds, and finish cooking in a 170 °C/340 °F for 5 minutes. Trim the half-spheres with a round cutter. To serve, count 3 half-spheres per serving. Fill the first and second one with the cream, cod's liver, and pea salad.
Scatter the cubed citron, peeled and crumbled grapefruit segments over this, add some oil and season with salt. Fill the third half-sphere with cream and peas. Arrange the three half-spheres together, and garnish with peas and vetch sprigs.

96 / P. 151
-

Cockle quenelle

The gustatory power of an aspic glaze.

1 kg cockles, 1 kg mussels, 1 onion, 1 shallot, 1,5 litre spring water, 500 g cream (35% butterfat), 2,5 g xanthan gum, 24 g dehydrated egg white, 1 bunch pilewort flowers, 15 cl white wine, 1 dash clear spirit vinegar, olive oil.

Wash and clean the cockles, soak them in cold salted water for 30 minutes to remove all sand. Drain, and repeat. Count 2 small cockles per serving and set them aside. Finely slice the shallot, sauté it in a little olive oil, and add the remaining cockles. Cover, stew on high heat until the cockles open, then deglaze with 5 cl white wine. Add 50 cl spring water, cook on medium heat for 10 minutes, then take off the heat, cover the pan with cling film and let sit for 1 hour. Strain and let cool. Clean and pick the mussels, stew them with the chopped onion until they're all open, deglaze with the remaining 10 cl white wine and the spirit vinegar. Strain the mussel juice and boil it down to 1/4. Boil down the cream by half, add 25 cl reduced mussel juice and the xanthan gum. Blend while still hot and let cool down to 50° C/122 °F. Pour it into a piping bag. Add the dehydrated egg white to 30 cl cockle broth, and whisk until firm. Spread the beaten egg whites in a roasting dish into a 7-cm thick layer. Cover with cling film, prick in several places, and cook at 80 °C/175 °F in a steam oven for 20 minutes. Put the reserved cockles in a frying pan, add a little water and heat until open.
Shell the cockles and clean the shells. Set aside 20 half-shells. Take the egg whites out of the oven. Shape them into quenelles, two per serving, and coat them with mussel-flavoured cream. Burn their top with a blowtorch. Put the cockles back into their half-shells and steam for a few seconds. Nestle the cockles into the egg whites, and stick some pilewort flowers into them.

97 / P. 163
-

Red root

Vinegared earth, the epitome of colour.

1 kg raw, round red beets, 2 g Metil, 1-1/2sheet gelatin, 1 head of broccoli, 1 sea bass (about 1 kg), 250 g balsamic vinegar, 20 g Algin, 2,5 g Gluco, 50 cl spring water, 100 g olive oil, 1 bunch purple cress, fleur de sel.

Bake half of the beets, wrapped in aluminium foil, for 2 hours at 180 °C/350 °F. Let cool, peel the beets and blend them into a fine puree. Extract the juice from the remaining beets through a juicer. Fillet the sea bass, leave the fillets to marinate in olive oil, covered with cling film. Blend 200 g pureed beets with the Metil. Soak the gelatin in cold water for 10 minutes. Heat 80 g beet juice and dissolve the drained gelatin in it.
Using a hand mixer, combine the beet puree and the beet juice, pour into a siphon and add a gas cartridge. Keep refrigerated.
Blend the spring water with the Algin, and use a sous-vide machine to eliminate air bubbles. Pour this water gel into a flat container.
Blend the balsamic vinegar with the Gluco and pour this into a squeeze bottle. Make small vinegar spheres in the water gel. Let sit for a few minutes, then rinse the spheres in water and set them aside in a little beet juice mixed with olive oil. Peel off the skin from the sea bass fillets, and cut them into cubes. On the plates, arrange the fish cubes, spacing them well. Season with fleur de sel. Dot each cube with a mound of beet foam, lifting the siphon's nozzle in order to leave a nice bird's beak on top of each mound. In the foam, stick a few shoots of purple cress, and generously grate some broccoli on the entire composition.
Serve a spoonful of spherified balsamic vinaigrette on the side.

98 / P. 47

-

Winter radish, burnt cauliflower

Strong, powerful, yet delicate.

1 litre milk, 4 long white radishes, 1 cauliflower, 1 litre milk, 16 heads of garlic, 20 g rapeseed oil, 1 kg butter, 15 g salt, 2 cl water.

Cook half the cauliflower in the milk. Drain, then blend in a Thermomix at speed 10 for 2 minutes. Halve the heads of garlic crosswise and cook them with the butter on very low heat for 1 hour. The garlic should be very tender, but still white. Rub thoroughly through a sieve. Mix this buttery garlic puree with the salt and water. Spoon into a piping bag. Clean the white radishes, discarding the frailer leaves. Halve lengthwise, then grate the bottom to obtain a flat surface. Scoop out the middle part of the radishes with an apple corer. Fill the radishes with the garlic-butter puree. Draw a shape with the cauliflower puree from the piping bag, making ends meet. At the last moment, lightly brown the filled radishes under a grill, humidifying the leaves to protect them from the heat. Place the radishes on the plates and grate the remaining half of cauliflower over them. Season with salt, and burn with a blow torch. Fill the inside of the cauliflower puree with rapeseed oil. Serve.

99 / P. 110

-

White radish, cuttlefish ink

A construction based on an instant marinade.

10 large white radishes, 30 g cuttlefish ink, 20 cl spring water, 1 400-g back cut of fresh cod fillet, 150 g coarse salt, white fish bones and trimmings, 250 g crème fraîche (35 % butterfat), 1 shallot, olive oil, fleur de sel.

With the shallot and fish bones and trimmings, make a fish stock, and boil it down to the demi-glace stage. Coat the cod fillet with coarse salt for 8 minutes, then rinse. Using a fine needle, prick the radishes on all sides and put them in sous-vide bags with a mix of spring water and cuttlefish ink. Seal the bags, vacuum, and leave to sit for 1 hour. Take out the radishes and rinse them in clear water. Cut them in quarters, making them all of the same height and with a flat bottom so that they stand upright. Stir the reduced fish stock into the crème fraîche, then add this to the juice from the sous-vide bag. Correct seasoning. Cook the radishes in a 80 °C/175 °F steam oven for 2 minutes. Cut the cod fillet into 6-mm thick slices and brush them with olive oil. Place the radishes upright on the plates, adjust the cod slices on top of them, and pour the sauce just before serving.

100 / P. 206

-

Pink radish, vinegared gel

1 Just like biting into the crispy radis, also finding the light sourness of a gel.

0 round pink radishes, 10 round radishes of various colours, 10 cl white wine vinegar, 20 g salt, 5 cl water, 5 sheets gelatin.

Halve the radishes. Mix the water, white wine vinegar and salt in a saucepan, and bring to a boil. Immediately throw the pink radishes into this preparation, take off the heat and marinate for 6 hours to obtain a pink stock. Soak the gelatin in cold water for 10 minutes. Pour out 1 litre of the pink stock into a saucepan, heat it and add the drained gelatin. Let cool until slightly thickened. Halve the radishes of various colours, keeping the leaves and roots on. Cover a large chunk of ice with a nonstick baking mat. Pour onto this a few drops of pink stock, then paste the cut side of a radish onto it. Leave to set for a few minutes, then gently lift the jelly with a spatula. Serve immediately.

101 / P. 124

-

Grapes, wood sorrel

Purple or wine-coloured, the vivaciousness of leaf and grain.

3 large clusters of white grapes, 20 stalks of purple wood sorrel (30 leaves), 2,5 g agar-agar, 0,5 g xanthan gum, spring water.

Pick 30 large berries from the clusters and peel them: put them in boiling water for 1 minute, then transfer them to a bath of lukewarm water and peel off the skin. Soak the grape skins in a little mineral water. Remove the seeds from the berries with a pair of tweezers. Extract the juice from the remaining grapes, stir in the agar-agar and bring to a boil. Refrigerate until set. Blend this jelly with the xanthan gum and spoon into a piping bag. To serve, drain the grapes, and wrap each one of them in 2 leaves of wood sorrel. Count 3 grapes per serving. Fill each wood sorrel cup with grape gel. Spray the plate with the drained mineral water in which the grape skins have been left to macerate.

102

-

Artichoke raviole

A tribute to Fulvio Pierangelini.

400 g all-purpose flour, 10 g maltodextrin, 10 large artichokes, 300 g butter, 62 g egg yolks, 2 frosted Tahiti vanilla pods, 50 g cream, 15 g peanut oil, 1 head garlic, 80 g milk, 2 g Iota, fine salt, olive oil, 20 cl spring water, 1 tbsp lemon juice.

Turn the artichokes; insert the hearts into a sous-vide bag with a dash of olive oil and lemon juice. Steam at 100 °C/212 °F from 30 minutes to 1 hour. Cool in iced water, discard the choke and blend. Take 200 g of this puree, blend it with the cream and 1,75 g fine salt. Spoon into a piping bag. Make a raviole dough — combine the flour, 150 g artichoke puree and the egg yolks in a stand mixer. Knead at speed 1 for 15 minutes, then wrap the dough in a sous-vide bag and refrigerate. Peel the garlic and parboil it 5 to 7 times in a row. Brown it lightly on a plancha with olive oil. Puree 100 g browned garlic with the mineral water, Iota and 2 g fine salt. Bring to a boil, let cool. Make a vanilla butter — slit and scrape the vanilla, add it to the milk and bring to a boil. Take off the heat, cover, and let cool. Knead 200 g butter, and gradually whisk in in the cold vanilla milk. Leave to cool. Add 3 g fine salt and the peanut oil to the vanilla milk, whisking well. Pour into a piping bag and set aside at room temperature. Place some of the artichoke leaves in a baking dish, cover with aluminium foil, and bake in a 200 °C/400 °F oven for 30 minutes. Add a little water, pour out the dark juice, and boil it down with maltodextrin until thickened. Set aside. Make the ravioles: roll out the dough 1,5 mm thick and cut out 11-cm disks. In the middle of each, place a little creamed artichoke puree, a knob of vanilla butter and a small mound of browned garlic jelly. Fold the ravioles in two, and seal the edges. Boil in water for 3 minutes, and drain. Drain the vanilla pods, and whisk the vanilla water into the remaining 100 g butter. Toss the ravioles in the vanilla butter and arrange them on the plates, pasting them with dots of artichoke jus.

103 / P. 116

-

Goat cheese raviole, bee pollen

Chewing an interrupted gesture and cooking process.

350 g pastry flour, 280 g egg yolks, 400 g semi-dry goat cheese, 100 g dried and powdered bee pollen, 250 g milk, 2,75 g agar-agar, fleur de sel, freshly ground pepper, 60 g frozen fresh rockrose bee pollen, 1 g xanthan gum, 150 g unsalted butter, 1 bunch orange African marigold flowers.

Combine the flour and egg yolks in a stand mixer and knead at speed 1 for 10 minutes. Put the dough in a sous-vide bag, vacuum, and refrigerate. Bring the milk and agar-agar to a boil, and leave to set. Break this jelly, stir in the fresh bee pollen and xanthan gum, season with salt, and blend with a hand mixer. Spoon into a piping bag. Make small balls of goat cheese, about 10 g each, by rolling them under your palm, then roll them into dried bee pollen. Make the ravioles : roll out the dough 1,5 mm thick, and cut out rectangles 15 cm long and 5 cm wide. On one half of each rectangle, place 2 two goat cheese balls 1,5 cm apart and 1,5 cm from the edge. Fold the raviole in two, sealing the entire length of the dough. Keep refrigerated on a bed of coarse semolina, then, at the last moment, boil in salted water for 4 minutes. Lift the ravioles out of the water with a slotted spoon and complete their cooking in foamy butter with the remaining dried bee pollen. On the plates, spread some fresh pollen cream and add the ravioles on either side. Decorate with African marigold petals and add some freshly ground pepper.

104 / P. 101

Greengage

A synchronized symbiosis of a plant and a fruit tree.

25 greengages, wild chervil, 10 pieces of candied bergamot orange (from domaine Cavalas), 10 fresh lime leaves, 14 lime leaves for infusion, 14 g dried lime blossoms, ascorbic acid, 450 g sugar, 20 g Algin, 16 g Calcic, 4 to 6 green peppercorns, 5 g olive oil, 2 g bergamot syrup, 2 g green peppercorn water, 1 dash vanilla extract.

Stone 15 greengages. In a low-rimmed saucepan, stew them on medium heat with 250 g sugar. Keep stewing until you get a thick compote. Blend with the green peppercorns, and rub through a sieve. Spoon into a piping bag. Boil 1 litre water with 200 g sugar, and add 7 g lime blossoms. Cover and let sit for 6 minutes. Let cool. In another saucepan, make the same syrup and steep the remaining lime blossoms in it. Let cool, then add the vanilla extract and 2,5 g ascorbic acid. Blend the first cold infusion with the Algin in a Thermomix at full power for 2 minutes. Transfer to a sous-vide bag and remove all air bubbles with the vacuum machine. Set aside. In two different containers, pour 1 litre water and stir in 8 g Calcic. Set aside. Have another container filled with cold water to rinse the spherifications. Put the remaining greengages in a 100 °C/212 °F steam oven for 1 minutes, then transfer the plums to a bath of iced water with a pinch of ascorbic acid added to it. Peel the greengages. (Tip : always keep them immersed to prevent oxidation.) Using an oyster knife, stone each greengage, trying to damage the fruit as little as possible : cut each fruit following its medium line and dislodge the stone, and replace it with a cube of bergamot orange. Drain for no more than 1 minutes to prevent oxidation.
Do the spherification : place a drained and stuffed greengage in the Algin bath, then transfer it to the Calcic bath. Repeat the process with all the greengages, leaving them in the gelling bath for 1 minute. Remove them from the bath, discard any asperities if needed, and return them to the Calcic bath for 1 more minute. Rinse. Keep the greengages in the second lime infusion (the one with the ascorbic acid and vanilla added) and set aside. Mix all the herbs — wild chervil, scented geranium and finely shredded lime leaf.
Make a vinaigrette by whisking together the green peppercorn water, bergamot syrup, and olive oil. To serve, spread a stain of greengage compote onto the plate, add one drained greengage, then another stain of greengage compote. Add the herbs and a little vinaigrette. Serve.

105 / P. 244

Rhubarb, birch

Rhubarb in all its sweetness and austerity.

2 kg large rhubarb sticks, 160 g cream, 80 g egg whites, 450 g sugar, 5 sheets gelatin, 50 g butter, 35 cl spring water, 1 cl birch sap infused with birch leaves, 100 g xylitol (birch sugar).

Soak the gelatin in cold water. Peel the rhubarb and stew half of it. When it has reduced and looks like a compote, weigh 400 g of it, add the butter and the drained gelatin, and stir until melted. Whip the cream to stiff peaks. Beat the egg whites with 50 g sugar in a stand mixer. Gently fold the whipped cream and the beaten egg whites into the rhubarb compote. Pour this into a straight-edged baking sheet in a 3-cm thick layer. Make a syrup with 25 cl water, 250 g sugar — bring to a boil and let cool. Cut the remaining rhubarb into thin slices, 1 mm thick, 15 cm long.
Cover most of the rhubarb slices with the syrup, and transfer them to a sous-vide bag and a sous-vide machine in order to soften them. Cut the remaining rhubarb slices in 2-cm squares. Toss them in the xylitol and dry them in a 50° C/122 °F dehydrator. Make a syrup by boiling the remaining 10 cl water with the remaining 150 g sugar. Add the birch water, and pour into a squeeze bottle. Cut the rhubarb mousse into cylinders with a 3-cm round cutter. Wrap these cylinders in the rhubarb strips, and keep refrigerated. Just before serving, arrange the rhubarb rolls on the plates, sprinkle with birch syrup, and decorate with the rhubarb crisps.

106 / P. 247
-

Rhubarb, bindweed

The rhubarb stalk as a prop for the bindweed.

15 large rhubarb stalks, with leaves on, 50 g butter, 1 kg sugar, 21,5 cl spring water, 250 g crème fraîche, 1 bunch of bindweed, 2 g ice cream stabilizer, 150 g peanut oil, 20 g maltodextrin.

Peel the rhubarb, and stew 10 of the stalks without sugar until soft, mashing it into a compote. Keep the remaining 5 stalks wrapped in a cloth and refrigerate. Weigh 500 g of stewed rhubarb compote and add the butter in small pieces, mixing until melted. Bring 16,5 cl spring water and 250 g sugar to a boil, adding the maltodextrin and stabilizer. Stir the rhubarb compote into the syrup, blend with a hand mixer and pour into a Pacojet bowl. Freeze until hard. Make another syrup with the remaining 5 cl water and 750 g sugar, and refrigerate until cold. Cut the remaining rhubarb stalks with a mandolin cutter into thin strips, 1,5-cm wide, 6-cm long and 2-mm thick. Keep refrigerated. Whip the cream to stiff peaks, making it as fluffy as you can. Make a rhubarb leaf oil — pick the youngest, greenest leaves and blend them with the peanut oil. Strain through a fine sieve. To serve, first make the sorbet in the Pacojet machine. Dip the raw rhubarb strips into the cold syrup, and run them through a sous-vide machine for 2 minutes. Drain and pile them up into stalks, five by five, pasting them with some whipped cream at the bottom so that they stand upright. Place them on the plates this way, add a scoop of sorbet on the side, sprinkle with some rhubarb leaf oil, and dot with a few bindweed leaves and some thinly shredded rhubarb kept in iced water until stiffened and curled-up.

107 / P. 252
-

Veal sweetbread in green sauce

A classic product, just grilled.

4 veal sweetbreads, 250 g each; 200 g spinach, 200 g smoked herring, 1 litre spring water, seasonal herbs.

Make a smoked herring stock — dice the herring fillets, sauté them briefly in olive oil, then add 1 litre spring water. Simmer for 20 minutes, then take off the heat, cover the saucepan with cling film, and let sit for 30 minutes. Strain the stock through a fine sieve. Pick, wash, drain the spinach, and cook them in the smoked herring stock. Drain again, and blend in a Thermomix until smooth. Set aside. Soak the sweetbreads in cold water for 24 hours. Drain and rinse. Blanch the sweetbreads in simmering water, without boiling, stirring all the while, for 2 to 3 minutes, then let cool and peel the sweetbreads. Sear them until lightly browned, then bake in a 170 °C/340 °F oven for 8 minutes on each side. Add the smoked spinach puree, and add a few fresh seasonal herbs.

108 / P. 39
-

Fried samphire balls

The crispy, salty, succulent herb of the seashore.

400 g young, tender samphire, 20 cl iced spring water, 150 g pastry flour, 1 egg yolk, oil for deep-frying.

Wash, drain the samphire and carefully pat dry. Make a tempura with the water, flour and egg yolk, without overworking the batter. Roll the samphire lightly in flour and add it, a few sprigs at a time, to the tempura batter in order to coat it well. Drain the samphire, shaping it into loose clusters. Deep-fry in 70 °C/340 °F oil, waiting until the fried samphire rises to the surface and separates slightly. Drain on kitchen paper and serve immediately.

109 / P. 158
-

Buckwheat, salt-cured lemon

A veil thrown onto a frozen buckwheat stone.

100 g dry buckwheat seeds, 4 salt-cured lemons, 1,425 litre milk, 110 g inverted sugar, 1 g ice cream stabilizer, 25 g dextrose, 20 g sugar, 5 g agar-agar, 1,5 sheet gelatin, 5 g dried egg whites.

Make the ice cream: lightly toast 45 g buckwheat seeds in a dry saucepan. Add 1 litre milk, then the dextrose, inverted sugar, and stabilizer. Cover and cook for 15 minutes. Blend with a hand mixer, and pour into a Pacojet bowl. Then, make the buckwheat jelly. Again, toast 25 g buckwheat seeds in a dry saucepan and add 25 cl milk. Off the heat, cover the saucepan with cling film and let cool. Strain the cold milk, collect the buckwheat from the sieve, and cook it until mushy in a little water. Pour the infused milk into a saucepan; add the agar-agar and 10 g sugar. Bring to a boil and pour this into very flat rimmed sheets, placed on a very horizontal surface, in a 1-mm layer. Leave to set.
Cut the jelly into 10-cm squares, lay them flat on a large, very smooth sheet of cling film, and leave in a ventilated walk-in cooler for a day. The jellly will dry to some extent, becoming plastic-like and easy to shape.
Scoop out the pulp and white part from the salt-cured lemons (keep them for another use), and dice the rind of one lemon very finely. Keep refrigerated. Leave the three remaining rinds in a dehydrator until dry, but do not wait until they take on a white color. Pulverize into a very fine powder. Finally, make the mousse — first, soak the gelatin in cold water. Toast the remaining 25 g buckwheat in the same manner as above, and deglaze with the remaining 17,5 cl milk. Cover the saucepan with cling film and let sit for 30 minutes. Strain, reheat gently to dissolve 10 g sugar and the gelatin in the preparation. Whisk in the dried egg whites, and beat to stiff peaks. Transfer the mousse to a container, and refrigerate. Plate this dish at the last moment before serving: put a square of jelly on the plate. Place a few salt-cured lemon cubes on the jelly, plus a few cooked buckwheat seeds, a spoonful of mousse and a large scoop of ice cream. Pick up the four corners of the jelly, join them together and turn the jelly over, giving it volume. Sprinkle with a little powdered salt-cured lemon.

110 / P. 238
-

Herb stalk soufflé

The boldness of an exercise in style – herb sap turned into a soufflé.

20 cl milk, 30 g egg yolk, 20 g corn flour, 100 g sugar, 15 g green Chartreuse, 150 g egg whites, 25 g unsalted butter, 1 bunch angelica, 1 bunch celery, 1 bunch wild chervil, 1 bunch young hogweed sprigs, 1 stalk rhubarb, 1 stick candied angelica, 1 poached/fermented hogweed stalk.

Make a pastry cream — boil the milk, take off the heat, cover. Whisk the egg yolks with 40 g sugar and the corn flour. Whisk in the milk, cook until thickened, then, off the heat, add the Chartreuse. Stir well, refrigerate until cold. Pluck out all the leaves from the herbs and plants, including the hogweed seeds. Run all of them through a juice extractor, collect all the herb juice, cover its surface with cling film and refrigerate. Separate the stalks in two equal-sized bunches. Finely dice one of them, whisk them with 30 g egg whites, mix well and set aside in ice cubes. Assemble the other bunch into a bundle, 15 to 20 cm high, tie it with string, and keep in damp kitchen paper. Store a soufflé dish or a 10-cm high, 10-cm wide copper saucepan in a deep-freezer until quite cold. Melt the butter and brush the inside of the cold vessel with it. Thin 150 g pastry cream with 2 tbsp green juice. Whisk the remaining 120 g egg whites with 60 g sugar until stiff. Gently fold this meringue into the herbed pastry cream, then fill the cold buttered vessel with it. Smooth the surface, then run your index finger all around the mould, separating some of the meringue from it. Bake in a 210 °C/410 °F fan oven for 15 minutes. Serve immediatly out of the oven — take the bundle of stalks out of the damp paper, halve it. Spoon out some of the soufflé crust and some of the inside, and stick the bundle into the hole. Serve with a spoonful of chilled diced stalks on the side.

111 / p. 249

Iced nettle soufflé

Taming and cooking the indigenous invader of the marsh.

45 cl 45-proof fruit brandy, 450 g sugar, 11,5 cl water, 5 sprigs nettle, 80 g egg yolks, 130 g egg whites, 300 g cream, 3 cl nettle brandy, 2 cl green Chartreuse, 30 g parsley, oil for deep-frying, a few leaves of white oleander.

Bring the fruit brandy and water to a boil with 50 g sugar. Pour this onto the nettles, cover, let cool and let sit for 5 days. Strain through a fine sieve. Whip the cream to soft peaks. Beat the egg whites with 200 g sugar until firm, then beat in 150 g more sugar and 15 cl water. Fold this into the whipped cream. Blend the parsley with a few drops of water until smooth. Fold this into the soufflé batter, and pour the batter into a soufflé dish. Deep-freeze for 3 hours. Mix the egg yolks, 50 g sugar and 1,5 cl water. Add the different brandies and liqueurs, including the nettle brandy. Coat the nettle leaves with a very small layer of batter, and deep-fry. Serve the soufflé with the tempura and a few white oleander leaves.

112 / p. 184

Winey spatula

An invitation to the grape harvest.

5 blood peaches, 10 cl syrah red wine, 25 g sugar, 1,25 g agar-agar, 50 g red grape juice, 10 green hazelnuts, 50 g hazelnut oil.

Stew 4 of the peaches, making sure all moisture is evaporated. Rub through a sieve. Weigh 100 g of this compote, stir in the red wine, grape juice, sugar, and agar-agar. Bring to a boil, then pour into a small rimmed tray lined with cling film. Peel and finely dice the remaining peach. Peel the green hazelnuts and finely slice them with a mandolin cutter. Cut the red wine jelly into strips, 5-cm long and 1.2 cm wide. Position them on angled spatulas, pasting them with a little peach compote. Arrange the diced peach on the jelly, and stick the hazelnut slivers into the jelly. Using a squeeze bottle, add a few drops of hazelnut oil.

113 / p. 197

Juices of scampi

A lace of concentrated taste.

About 25 langoustine heads, 40 g agar-agar, 1 tbsp tomato puree, olive oil, 1,5 l water.

Brown the langoustine heads in a large pan with a dash of olive oil. Add the tomato puree, and stir, crushing the langoustine heads. Add the water and simmer for 45 minutes. Rub through a sieve. Mix 1 litre of this broth with the agar-agar, and leave to set. Cut the resulting jelly into chunks and grate them onto parchment paper with a coarse Microplane grater. Leave in a dehydrator until quite dry.

114 / P. 265
-

Chicken, lemon verbena

A mellow infusion.

5 large farm-raised chicken breasts, 2 bunches lemon verbena, 8 flat peaches, 1 litre semi-skimmed milk, 2 g sucrose esters, 200 g unsalted butter, fleur de sel, pepper.

Dry the leaves of 1 bunch lemon verbena in a dehydrator. Pulverize in a blender. Butterfly the chicken breasts and lay them flat on cling film. In the middle of each butterflied chicken breast, align some fresh verbena leaves, then fold back the chicken and roll it very tightly into the film. Insert into sous-vide bags, vacuum, and cook in a Roner at 56 °C/133 °F for 1 hour. Melt the butter, add the leaves of another half-bunch of verbena, and leave to infuse. Set aside a few fresh tops from the remaining half-bunch of verbena, pluck out the leaves and make a lemon verbena emulsion : heat the milk to 20 °C, add the verbena leaves, cover with cling film and leave to infuse for 1 hour. Strain, season with salt and add the sucrose esters. Slice 3 of the flat peaches, cut the remaining 5 into random-sized bits, and bake them with a little verbena butter. Season with salt and pepper. Take the chicken breasts from the sous-vide bags, pat them dry and gently brown them in the verbena butter. Trim the chicken breasts and cut them in two. Season with salt and pepper. To serve, arrange the roasted peaches on the plates, spacing them a bit. Sprinkle with verbena powder and fresh shoots, then add the chicken with its cooking butter and the verbena emulsion.

115 / P. 253
-

Wood sorrel stalks, capers

Almost nothing – a stalk, a powder. But an exciting point to start from.

1 bunch chervil, 10 large wood sorrel stalks, 250 g capers in vinegar, olive oil.

Drain the capers and leave them to dry in a dehydrator. When completely dry, pulverize them in a blender and sieve the powder. Trim the chervil stalks into neat, regular bundles, and tie them with a piece of string so that they stand upright.
Pluck out the wood sorrel leaves and keep them for another use. Dip them lightly in olive oil, then roll them in the powdered capers and stick them into the bundle of chervil stalks in a loop shape. Serve as a first mise en bouche.

116 / P. 169
-

Horn tomato, sea bream

Like a Norman-Picard version of a ceviche.

1,5 kg horn tomatoes, 2 sea breams, 1 bunch red-veined sorrel, 1 bunch wild cress, olive oil, fleur de sel, freshly ground pepper, 5 g agar-agar, 2,5 g Algin, 15 g Calcic, 1 litre spring water, 2 cloves garlic.

Peel the tomatoes. Dry the skins in a dehydrator and blend them to a powder. Set aside 2 of the largest ones and coarsely chop the others. Stew them in a covered pan with the crushed garlic, on low heat, for 1 hour. Let cool, strain through a sieve, and set aside the tomato water. Slow-roast half of the pulp in a 120 °C/248 °F for an hour and a half. Set aside. Measure 25 cl tomato water, and blend it with the Algin. In another vessel, blend the spring water with the Calcic. Using a caviar box, make tomato pearls with the tomato solution dropped into the Calcic bath. Stir the agar-agar into 50 cl tomato water. Season with salt, bring to a boil. Pour into a rectangular 35 x 15 cm silicone tray to a thickness of 2 mm. Refrigerate until set, keeping the tray horizontal. Fillet the sea bream, peel off the skin, and finely slice the fillets. Lay the slices on the entire surface of 6 jellies, aligning them with the edges. In the same manner, cover 3 jellies with dried tomato pulp, in a 4-mm thick layer. Arrange the jellies into a stack, with a tomato pulp jelly at the bottom, in the middle and at the top. Refrigerate for 1 hour. Cut this tomato millefeuille into 1,5 cm wide slices, and leave them at room temperature. Using a ham slicer, finely slice the 2 remaining raw tomatoes lengthwise to a thickness of 1,5 mm. Lay a tomato slice flat on a plate, and carefully adjust a slice of millefeuille on its narrower side onto the entire length of the tomato.

Season with fleur de sel, pepper, and olive oil. Dress the composition with shoots and sorrel and cress. Sprinkle some tomato powder on the back of the composition, and just before serving, add the tomato pearl, seasoned with salt and olive oil.

117 / P. 114

-

Pineapple tomato, sea bass

The flesh of a fruit, lengthwise, crosswise and otherwise.

10 large pineapple tomatoes, 400 g sea bass fillets, 5 g xanthan gum, 10 cl water, bear's garlic flowere, salt, pepper.

Parboil and peel the tomatoes, setting the skins aside. Cut the 2 firmest tomatoes into 2 mm slices. Mix the water and salt to make brine, add the sliced tomatoes and the skins, and dry for 2 hours in a dehydrator at 60 °C/140 °F. The tomatoes should be dry, but not browned. Quarter the remaining tomatoes, setting aside the seeds. Insert half of the seeds into a sous-vide bag, make vacuum, and leave them in a steam oven at 80 °C/175 °F for an hour and a half. Set aside the remaining seeds. Stir the xanthan gum into 10 cl water. Lay the tomato slices between 2 tea towels. Finely slice the sea bass fillets into carpaccio. Alternate layers of dried tomato and sliced sea bass in a 5-cm wide round cutter. Put the cutter and its contents in a sous-vid bag and make vacuum in order to compress it. Remove from bag, put on plate, and remove cutter. Decorate with tomato seeds, season with salt and pepper, and partially cover with dried tomato slices and skins. Add a few dots of tomato gel and decorate with bear's garlic flowers.

118 / P. 231

-

Tomato, powdered pig

Animal semolina.

5 kg oval-shaped yellow cherry tomatoes, 500 g yellow beets, 5 cl white balsamic condiment, 5 cl white wine, 5 cl water, 4 g xanthan gum, 2 kg pork skins, oil for deep-frying.

Boil the pork skins in water for an hour, longer if needed, skimming regularly throughout the cooking process. Cool in cold water, drain and scrape as much fat from the inside of the skins. Cut the skins into 20 cm squares and put them in a 75 °C/167 °F dehydrator for 12 to 15 hours. Leave outdoors for one day, then deep-fry at 195 °C/383 °F. Make sure the vessel is large enough and you are using enough oil, for the skins puff up considerably when deep-fried. Let cool, pat dry carefully, and blend by successive pulses in a Thermomix until you get a fine powder. With the tip of a knife, draw a cross at the stalk end of the tomatoes, scoop out the inside and set aside all the seeds. Peel the beets and finely dice them. Boil the white balsamic condiment, water, and white wine, and pour them over the raw beets. Let sit for 1 hour. Drain, collect 10 cl of juice, add the xanthan gum, and blend with a hand mixer. Make the 'stuffing' : mix the diced beets, tomato seeds, and vinegared gel. Stuff 6 small tomatoes per serving. To serve, place the tomatoes upright, and add a generous spoonful of powdered pig skin.

119 / P. 233
-

Jerusalem artichoke in a sugared almond crust

A root vegetable, so close to a fruit.

8 Jerusalem artichokes, 25 g egg white, 50 g ground almonds, 200 g ground sugared almonds, 67,5 cl milk, 390 g Jerusalem artichokes, 100 g egg yolks, 40 g glucose, 2 g ice cream stabiliser, 105 g sugar, 5 g candied bergamot syrup (domaine Cavalas), 1 g hazelnut oil, 40 g grapeseed oil, the seeds of 1/4 vanilla pod, 3 lemons, 6,5 g agar-agar, 150 g sorrel.

Wash the 8 Jerusalem artichokes, wrap them in aluminium foil, and bake them at 180 °C/350 °F for 25 minutes. Leave to cool, and peel. Mix the egg white, ground almonds and 170 g ground sugared almonds. Wrap the Jerusalem artichokes in this dough, and bake at 175 °C/347 °F on a baking sheet lined with parchment paper. Wash the 390 g Jerusalem artichokes, set one aside, cook the others in boiling salted water, and peel. Blend them to a puree, add 30 cl milk, and blend until smooth. Bring to a boil with the glucose and stabilizer. Take off the heat. Whisk the sugar with the egg yolks whisk in the artichoke milk, and cook, stirring, until thickened. Blend and rub through a sieve. Let cool and refrigerate overnight. Pour into a Pacojet bowl and freeze until solid. Peel the remaining Jerusalem artichoke, dice it finely, add the juice of 2 lemon and put into a sous-vide bag. Vacuum. Bring to a boil 37,5 cl milk, the juice of a lemon, sugar and agar-agar. Let cool, then add the sorrel leaves and blend. Strain through a fine sieve and spoon into a piping bag. On a wooden serving board, place the Jerusalem artichoke in its crust. In a bowl, place the artichoke ice cream. Break the artichoke's crust and place it beside the ice cream. Mix the oils, bergamot syrup, and vanilla seeds, and pipe the sorrel cream onto the pieces of crust.

120 / P. 131
-

Black trumpet mushrooms, lichen

An edible Japanese garden.

1 kg black trumpet mushrooms, 500 g white bread, 100 g cuttlefish ink, fresh lichen, butter.

Thoroughly clean the mushrooms, making sure no impurities are left. Toast the bread. Mix the cuttlefish ink with a little water, bring to a boil. Soak the bread in the ink, and leave for 24 hours in a dehydrator.
Put the bread in a Thermomix and pulverize it. Sauté the mushrooms in butter for 1 minutes, divide them between the plates, cover with black breadcrumbs and stick a few sprigs of lichen into the crumbs.

121 / P. 78
-

Milky milk-fed veal

A porcelain of brine and veal.

1 kg veal rump, 25 cl water, 12 medium-sized oysters, 2 white turnips, 500 g black radish, 500 g fresh cheese, tansy and red pimpernel sprigs, 7 g xanthan gum, olive oil.

Shuck the oysters, collecting their water, and finely dice the flesh. Blend the oyster water with 6 g xanthan gum, and set aside about 100 g of this for the oyster cream. Finely chop the veal with a knife, and mix it with the oysters. Keep refrigerated. Peel the turnips and finely slice them with a ham slicer.
Put them in a sous-vide bag with a little olive oil, and run them through a sous-vide machine. Using a 6-cm round cutter, cut out disks from the turnip slices. Make the oyster cream : blend the oyster water with the fresh cheese, adding the remaining xanthan gum. Cover a 4-cm round cutter with a slice of turnip. Place a knob of the veal and oyster tartare, press down, and cover with another slice of turnip.
Count two ravioles of this type per serving.
To serve, lay 2 ravioles on top of each other, like a small plate on a larger plate. Brush with the oyster cream. Garnish with red pimpernel sprigs and one tansy sprig.

122 / P. 122
-
Beet vermicelli

Angel red hair.

10 round red beets, oil for deep-frying, fleur de sel.

Peel the beets and shred them into vermicelli with a Japanese turning cutter. Keep each shredded beet separate. Heat the oil to 140 °C/284 °F, pick up the shredded beets one by one, shaping the vermicelli into a bunch, and drop them into the hot oil. Raise the temperature to 155 °C/131 °F. Once the foam has disappeared from the vermicelli, let them rise to the surface and keep frying at 150 °C/300 °F until dry. Lift them out, pat them dry with kitchen paper without crushing them, season with salt, and serve warm on a folded cloth.

123 / P. 75
-
Puffball

Rare and short-lived, before the dust cloud stage.

50 young puffballs, 1 cauliflower, 1 litre milk, 10 cl sunflower oil, 1 vanilla pod, 5 cloves garlic, 400 butter, burnt bread powder, salt.

Make sure the puffballs are very young : when they are too old, the inside is porous. Clean the stalks, then keep the mushrooms in a bow on a layer of wet kitchen paper. Cut the cauliflower into chunks and cook it in boiling milk for 20 minutes. Drain, puree in a blender, season with salt and store in a piping bag. Refrigerate. Make a vanilla oil : blend the oil and the seeds from the vanilla pod. Dry the pod in a dehydrator. Make the garlic crisps : using a truffle mandolin, finely slice the garlic cloves and deep-fry them at 150 °C/300 °F until golden. To serve, shortly before serving, heat some butter until foamy. Add the dried vanilla pod, then the mushrooms, and sauté for a few minutes. Draw five lines of cauliflower puree on each plate using a spatula. Add the mushrooms, decorate them with garlic crisps, and season with salt and vanilla oil. Sprinkle with two pinches of burnt bread powder *(see Black trumpet, lichen).*

124 / P. 44
-
Elderflower vinegar

Catching a smell, a taste in a net, like a perfumer.

500 g elderflowers, 2 litres white balsamic condiment, 30 cl water, 100 g sugar.

Leave a 3-litre Mason jar or Le Parfait jar for 15 minutes in a 100 °C/212 °F steam oven to sterilize it. Bring the balsamic condiment, water and sugar to a boil. Put the elderflowers into the jar, cover them with the boiling liquid, then immediately close the jar. You may use the vinegar after an hour, but keeping it for up to one year deepens the flavours.

Acknowledgments

The Canche, which borders *La Grenouillère*, flows inexorably on. It reminds me of my status as a simple custodian of this place. At each moment, in its constant movement, this discrete river reminds me of the time that's slipping away from me.

Year after year, *La Grenouillère* continues to benefit from loyal customers, supporters and friends. I warmly thank them all here.

Roland, my father, has become a protective figure who advises and reassures me. His role is crucial.

Patrick Bouchain is a guiding light in beauty, work and friendship. *La Grenouillère* today would not exist without him. His keen perspective continues to guide me.

With me for eight years, Lizzie Girard has become my right-hand woman. She was nineteen years old when she arrived and has progressed with talent. She's now ready to take flight and I'm delighted for her. She will make her own way and, I have no doubt, will leave her mark.

Emmanuel Roux, Felix Robert and Alix Marquant keep the kitchens at *La Grenouillère* bubbling with creativity. They have kept the pace going with style and loyalty for many years. I thank them for it.

It's up to Magali, Virginie, Jérôme and Samuel at *Anecdote* and *Froggy's* to manage the teams and the workloads with the necessary metronomic precision and without dissent. Bravo ladies and gentlemen!

I have been fortunate that talented men have been willing to look at my career. They have become friends and their advice is precious to me. Thanks to Alex Croquet, exceptional baker; Laurent Petit, sound cook; Olivier Roellinger, extraordinary chef and hotelier; Michel Guérard, mastermind of French cuisine for several generations.

Artists daily boost my soul and spirit. I'm thinking here of Annette Messager, who kindly wrote the preface to this book. I thank her for her very personal and sincere words.

I also think of Robert Combas, my friend Bartabas and, of course, Georges Rousse, who 'took over' *La Grenouillère*. I'm also thinking of Bruno Mantovani, Johann Le Guillerm and Julien Gosselin. It's good to be close to them.

My cultural journey owes a lot to Jérôme Bouvet, Agathe Fontaine and Michael Bouvier. They have helped me to understand, discover, schedule and produce.

I think also of Francis Peduzzi, our friend from the Channel. I would like to thank here some precious friends who surround *La Grenouillère* with their goodwill. Thanks to Francis Senet and to Claude, Sylvie and Philippe Kernanet and François Mortreux for their presence and their support from day one. They are my guardian angels.

I don't forget the voices of Clotaire Spanneut, Henri Bebey, Frédéric Brun and Alexandre Merveille. Each, in their way, manage *La Grenouillère* and help me make decisions.

I love working with the Japanese architect Kinya Maruyama, who enchants us with his drawings and his smile; whith Harumi and Takashi Osawa, they all became my friends from rising sun; with Syl, our ceramist, who transforms my ideas as I do hers; with Adrien Gosselin, whose work in *La Grenouillère*'s gardens enchants this place between ramparts and marshes.

My warm thanks go to my kitchen and restaurant staff for the passion and motivation they bring to a demanding job. They come and go — our profession is like that — but they put all their heart and energy into it.

This book owes a lot to Joséphine Lacasse, who knows how to tightrope with talent; to Laurent Seminel who created the design and offered me a heartfelt text; to Jean-Christophe Planche, a friend to share secrets with; to Ryoko Sekiguchi, for his poetry and talent; and to Nicolas Chatenier, the observant friend of the circle. Laurent and Nicolas have been with me from the start. They are the well-informed witnesses of the busy life of *La Grenouillère*.

Marie Pierre Morel has long been the official photographer of the seasons of *La Grenouillère*. For years, she has been focussing her camera and her gaze on my work and my region. With finesse and precision, she manages to reveal and say what I see and feel. Thank you.

Here, I think warmly of my mother, Claudine Filez, my brother, Guillaume Gauthier, and the rest of my family who, from afar, follow my career closely. And not forgetting my little sister Lulu.

I have the joy of sharing my greatest pride with Magali: my son Eustache, 7 years old now. He makes his way in life, as he does in my life; he is a joy that fills me day after day.

Finally, as this second book comes to an end, I want to say how deeply I feel like the child of a region. That of La Madelaine-sous-Montreuil and Montreuil-sur-Mer, a region bordered by the ramparts of Vauban and the Canche, filled with memories, trials and joys. Rooted in this territory, the Opal Coast, I continue to shape my life.